The World of Cities

21ˢᵀ-CENTURY SOCIOLOGY

SERIES EDITOR: Steven Seidman, State University of New York at Albany

The *21ˢᵗ-Century Sociology* series provides instructors and students with key texts in sociology that speak with a distinct sociological voice and offer thoughtful and original perspectives. The texts reflect current discussions in and beyond sociology, avoiding standard textbook definitions to engage students in critical thinking and new ideas. Prominent scholars in various fields of social inquiry combine theoretical perspectives with the latest research to present accessible syntheses for students as we move further into the new millennium amidst rapid social change.

Already published:

Forthcoming:

The World of Cities

Places in Comparative and Historical Perspective

ANTHONY M. ORUM AND XIANGMING CHEN

Blackwell Publishing

BLACKWELL PUBLISHING
350 Main Street, Malden, MA 02148-5020, USA
9600 Garsington Road, Oxford OX4 2DQ, UK
550 Swanston Street, Carlton, Victoria 3053, Australia

First published 2003 by Blackwell Publishing Ltd

3   2005

Library of Congress Cataloging-in-Publication Data has been applied for.

ISBN-13: 978-0-631-21025-2 (hardback)
ISBN-10: 0-631-21025-3 (hardback)
ISBN-13: 978-0-631-21026-9 (paperback)
ISBN-10: 0-631-21026-1 (paperback)

A catalogue record for this title is available from the British Library.

Set in 10 on 12 pt Photina
by Ace Filmsetting Ltd, Frome, Somerset
Printed and bound in the United Kingdom
by TJ International, Padstow, Cornwall

The publisher's policy is to use permanent paper from mills that operate a sustainable
forestry policy, and which has been manufactured from pulp processed using acid-free and
elementary chlorine-free practices. Furthermore, the publisher ensures that the text paper
and cover board used have met acceptable environmental accreditation standards.

For further information on
Blackwell Publishing, visit our website:
www.blackwellpublishing.com

Contents

Illustrations

Plates

Figures

Tables

Chart

Map

Preface

This is a book about cities. We shall introduce you to the basic ideas about cities, different ways of looking at cities, as well as how cities vary from one epoch to another, and from one society to another. We will rely on many specific examples of cities in this book, for instance, London and New York, Chicago and Shanghai, and we will generally assume that all these cities are very much alike.

But, of course, they are not. Cities differ in terms of the size of their populations, the size of their territory, as well as of their economic functions and cultural features. Some are what we would call a large metropolis, while others are simply small cities or towns. Some have a history that stretches back many hundreds of years – like London and Paris, while others have been around for only a few decades, like Naperville, Illinois. The miraculous growth of the Chinese city of Shenzhen bordering Hong Kong over the past two decades has earned it the title of "the city built overnight." We hope that you will appreciate our somewhat eclectic use of these different examples to convey the nature of city life, but we choose to do so to provide you a rich and broad sense of what cities are all about.

Once we get beyond our examples and illustrations, the waters become a bit murkier. There are different ideas about how cities work and about how they develop over time. There are also different ways for focusing on the residents of cities and the manner of their lives. Because we believe it important, in an advanced textbook such as this, to give you as catholic a view of theory as of the city, itself, we discuss, albeit briefly, different ways for thinking about cities and how they work. This broad and systematic treatment of urban theories distinguishes our book from introductory level texts on urban studies. Some of these ideas are grounded in the writings of great social theorists, as, for instance, those of Karl Marx. But some are of more recent vintage, such as the analyses and provocative ideas of the sociologist, Saskia Sassen, who argues about the deep and transforming nature of the forces of the global economy today.

While we have tried to give you a fair and concise picture of these different theories, we have refrained from giving a single endorsement to any perspective. We, ourselves, tend to differ in our perspectives. Orum tends to an historical view of the development of cities, and tries to emphasize economic and political forces in his own work. Chen, by contrast, tends to work on more recent cities, especially those in the Pacific Rim, such as in China, and he tends to emphasize mainly the global economic and cultural forces. Together we bring different but comparative and complementary perspectives and evidence to bear on cities. While we emphasize the ways that the growth of the economy or the forces of government shape the development of cities, we try also to give a fair overview of the historical development of cities in the United States, more or less free of a single theoretical perspective. Such an historical discussion is intended to introduce you to the major ways that American cities have developed, but does not especially adhere to only a single theoretical lens through which to tell that story. In our writing about China, we not only emphasize the interaction between the global economy and local government autonomy, but also demonstrate the importance of local cultural traditions and elements in the making of the modern city.

To date, the dominant story about the development of cities, especially over the past two centuries or so, has been a story of the deep and pervasive influence of economic and political institutions – of capitalism, in particular, and of the role of powerful officials within cities. Nevertheless, as we learn more about cities, we have come to recognize the important national and cultural differences among them. The cultural frame of reference, in fact, today has become increasingly popular as a way to understand the modern city, and is visibly evident in the writings of sociologists like Sharon Zukin. In addition, in our new age, of information and high technology, whole sets of new forces have begun to shape city life, among them, the computer and the Internet. These relatively new inventions, of just the past several decades, now make it far more possible for people to communicate with one another at great speeds and over major distances. The effects are quite noticeable, from reshaping the nature of the economies of large, global cities, like London or Tokyo, to the apparent liberation of people from working in specific sites and locations.

But while these changes have taken place, and many of their consequences are only now unfolding, we want to emphasize that there remains something very enduring and powerful about cities, which always experience both changes and continuities simultaneously (see chapters 3 and 4). They are the places where people are located in large numbers, and where they are often densely packed together. People gravitate to cities because they provide the nodes where new economies flourish and enterprises develop.

Beyond this, however, cities take on a meaning, a life all their own. They become, as we shall argue forcefully in chapter 1, ***places – specific sites in space where the lives and work of people are regularly conducted***. Moreover, within these large places, there are smaller ones, places like neighborhoods and homes to which we ourselves become tied. And therein, in the midst of these various layers of places, we find our own identities and personalities shaped, the foundations for communities of people among whom we live, a central dynamic to who we are as human beings. Cities, as places, in other words, are more than simply material facts of existence; they represent the social forms that serve to make us who we are.

An Overview of the Book

In the following five chapters of this book, then, we shall try to convey to you some of the richness and interest we have found in studying cities over the past couple of decades. Chapter 1 will introduce you to the concept of "place," suggesting how and why it is important to understanding the nature of cities. We also will distinguish this concept from other similar concepts, such as that of "space." Chapter 2 then turns to consider a number of different theoretical perspectives on the nature of cities. The ideas of Karl Marx figure large in many of these perspectives, even though he, himself, did not develop ideas specifically tailored to the nature and meaning of cities. We offer a number of different viewpoints, ranging from the work of Henri Lefebvre, a French Marxist, who developed ideas about the importance of space and social life, to those of Saskia Sassen, who takes a new global point of view about cities, suggesting how and why new social forces have emerged in them. While other introductory texts may avoid giving an overview of these many diverse theoretical perspectives, we offer it to prompt you to assess these perspectives further in light of our examples and other evidence. In chapter 3, we trace the history of metropolitan growth and development in the United States, from the late eighteenth century to the present. We show how the metropolis grew over time, and how the growth of suburbs mushroomed in the years following World War II. We also show how inequalities became deeply ingrained into the fabric of the American metropolis, resulting in the growth of a large urban underclass in the 1960s and 1970s. Finally, we suggest ways that gender differences make a difference to urban life, drawing on the writings of some prominent feminist scholars.

Chapter 4 then introduces you to a broad global, comparative view of cities today, especially those in China, with continued reference to such US cities as Chicago. We begin with a comparative discussion on how the global economy has begun to transform cities, making many of them, especially those in previously closed economic systems like China, highly vulnerable to external forces. Then we examine why and how local governments have become more autonomous under decentralization, which tends to make cities more entrepreneurial and competitively oriented, with both positive growth outcomes and potential undesirable consequences. We also discuss how the penetration of global commerce and consumerism and local traditions have created a new and hybrid cultural landscape, especially in such Chinese cities as Shanghai. We end chapter 4 by focusing on the direct and indirect spatial consequences of the global–local interaction in both the Chinese and American metropolitan contexts. And we conclude the book, in chapter 5, by showing ways in which cities might be improved. We extend our ideas of place as a means of talking about how cities, as places, could be reconstructed so as to improve the lives of their residents. We also discuss some of the newer ideas about how to refashion cities, including those of a group of people known as the New Urbanists. They work hard, among other things, to limit the influence of the automobile on the nature of community life within cities; and yet, for all their imagination, much of their work has been devoted to improving the lives of relatively wealthy residents in upscale villages and towns.

Please join us, then, as we take you on a journey, across time and space, over the urban landscape.

To help readers, especially students, with our text, we have employed several conventions. First, we have included a Glossary that contains all the important terms and concepts used throughout the book. These same Glossary terms then are highlighted in bold in the text. We also have set in bold italic certain terms and phrases that are essential to our arguments at particular places in the text. And, finally, we have set in roman italic certain words that are, by convention, set in that format.

Acknowledgments

Our work and completion of this book has been helped by a number of people and institutions. Orum wishes to thank the Great Cities Institute at the University of Illinois at Chicago for providing some time when he could work on the initial stages of the manuscript. In addition, he is grateful to a number of colleagues who provided some early reactions, among them, Judith Friedmann, Isaac Balbus, Kathleen Crittenden, James Norr, Amanda Lewis, and Kevin Fox Gotham. We are also very grateful to two reviewers who gave us comments. They are: Judith Friedmann and Sharon Zukin. Chen would like to acknowledge the partial support of the Chiang Ching-kuo Foundation for International Exchange for his collection of field data in Shanghai, some of which have been incorporated into the book. Chen also thanks Mr. Jiaming Sun for producing the map for chapter 4 and locating some scholarly material. All these people are to be thanked for the many improvements they suggested in the manuscript. Naturally, they are not responsible (nor would they want to be) for any errors of fact or interpretation which remain.

CHAPTER ONE

Cities and Places

To be (at all) is to be in (some) place. *Archytas of Tarentum*[1]

There is for virtually everyone a deep association with and consciousness of the places where we were born and grew up, where we live now, or where we have had particularly moving experiences. *Edward Relph*[2]

Of all the experiences we have in life, those that we have of cities may be among our most rich and enduring. Cities teem with the noise and clutter of human existence. Children shout, garbage cans bang, taxis honk their horns (though not too often any more), people pound the pavement, and cranes stretch through and over the sky. Cities are emphatic presences. They expose themselves to all our senses, and they leave us with deep impressions. And many of us find our own niches within them, the site of what we come to call home and ours. In this chapter, we want to discuss some of the basic notions that furnish the building blocks for how urban sociologists grapple to understand cities, and other human settlements, today.

We want to begin at the beginning, from the ground up, from the most obvious facts. What are cities after all? Why should they matter to us, both as human beings and as social scientists? Is it simply that they are composed of large numbers of people? Is it because they are locations where the work of moden civilization occurs? Or is there something else that makes cities, and their contents, so significant to us? We believe there is. And we shall argue in this chapter that cities, and similir human settlements, are significant to our lives essentially because they represent *places – that is, specific locations in space that provide an anchor and a meaning to who we are*. It is this quality of cities – this sense of their placeness and our own connection to places – that is one of the most fundamental, but also most unacknowledged, concepts of urban social science.[3]

Because we believe that the concept of place is so significant to understanding cities, we want to explore its nature at length and how it bears on our human experience throughout this first chapter. Though place may seem at first sight to be a trivial idea, nothing, we believe, could be further from the truth. Indeed, there is a growing recognition among many scholars, not just sociologists, that place is a central concept in the analysis of urban and regional areas, and how they are constructed and come to have meaning for their residents.[4] And though it may appear to be substantially less a notion than, let us say, consciousness, it surely bears an equally heavy weight on our existence and experience. And that is precisely why we shall devote some much-needed attention to it here, in an effort to secure it as a viable and independent concept.

Two Glimpses of Places

Let us begin our journey to the notion of place by looking at two actual places. The first is a village in the Philippines.[5] Here, some years ago, a volcano had erupted with great force and vengeance, sending villagers below it scattering to escape its destructive powers. The volcano roared for many days, showering former villages with ash and sparks, creating massive destruction in the huts and structures that once housed many residents. After a few weeks, the volcano died down; and after a few months, villagers were able to return to their old homes. With the massive amounts of lava and crusted ash that had been left on the ground, it would have seemed to make considerably more sense for the villagers simply to rebuild elsewhere. Pictures of the old village reveal a place that had been almost leveled, leaving bare traces of houses and stores that had once existed.

But, in fact, the villagers returned to their old village and began to reassemble the pieces of their lives by reassembling the village structures themselves. Now, note that the old buildings have been virtually completely buried by the ash. What once had been a large and vibrant church setting now is barely visible above the ground. A two or three story church is but a half story church; the local grocery store shared a similar fate.

In a remarkable feat of testimony to the strength of their community, the villagers returned to the place where that community had been. They took up their lives in the half-structures, reassembling the pieces of their religious life around the visible portions of the old church. They did the same with their remaining huts. While many had been destroyed, a few remained somewhat intact, portions sticking themselves out of the ground. Here, then, was a large group of villagers who, despite the assaults of nature, remain deeply attached to their sense of settlement. What had been their home remained so. What to us might have seemed simply like the vacant shell of a community was still a place to which they wanted to return.

One other place is important for our brief tour. This is another locale, one far more vivid in the history books than the tiny Philippine village. In 1991, the Soviet Union collapsed, imploding as the result of many internal and ex-

Plate 1.1 *Oblique View of San Guillermo Parish Church Prior to Eruption of Mt. Pinatubo in 1991.* Courtesy of Kathleen Crittenden. Reproduction of the photograph of the Church on display at the San Guillermo Museum.

Plate 1.2 *Direct View of San Guillermo Parish Church, Now Half Buried under Layers of Lahars, Near the End of 1995.* The Church has now been buried by many layers of lahars, or flowing mixtures of volcanic ash and water. Over six meters of volcanic ash settled in and around the Church. Courtesy of the Philippine Institute of Volcanology and Seismology.

Plate 1.3   *La Naval festival, San Guillermo Parish Church, November 2001.* Townspeople
arriving for local mass during La Naval festival. Courtesy of Kathleen Crittenden.

ternal problems. The fall of the Soviets was rather swift, taking many people
by surprise. Old Soviet generals tried to prevent the collapse, clinging to their
power in the only way that generals might. But they failed, and ultimately,
under the careful eye of Mikhail Gorbachev – the inventor of *glasnost* and
perestroika – the Soviet Union ended. There were many visible portraits of
the end, but no picture perhaps so enduring nor so strong as that of
Gorbachev's eventual successor, Boris Yeltsin, standing in Red Square, calling for an end to the Soviet Union and to the Communist Party.

When the television newscasts and the newspapers ran the story of the
demise of the Soviet Union, the picture of Yeltsin in Red Square provided a
banner declaration. There he was, surrounded by his followers, proclaiming
the death to Communism. Now it was only fitting that Yeltsin should proclaim the end of Communism in Red Square. For Red Square had become *the
central place* from which to celebrate the achievements and the victories of
the Soviet regime. Every year, on the first of May, the Soviet leaders had
brought out the military forces and the tanks, and the great personages, from
Stalin to Gorbachev, had overseen the flow of Soviet might before them. Battalion after battalion, troop after troop, tank after tank, marched across the
Square, signaling the great power that was the USSR.

What better location to tell the world of the end of the Soviet regime? And to do so in the midst of the chaos that reigned in Moscow? Red Square was the very heart and soul of the nation. A dagger to the heart and soul of the nation, delivered by its Prince Valiant, inevitably had to be delivered in Red Square.

In each of these two locales, then, place assumed a special significance for residents. It represented, in the first case, the home of a group of people, and the anchor of the community for its residents. And in the second, it provided the main public gathering spot and the site for the celebration of a whole nation and its accomplishments – its alpha and omega, its beginning and end.

The Foundations of Place

A BRIEF PHILOSOPHICAL OVERVIEW

In order to provide an absolutely firm foundation to our discussion of cities, and of urban sociology, we must have a full and complete appreciation of the notion of place. Here we do not simply refer to physical places that present themselves to us, as viewers and listeners, as buildings and monuments and streets, for example. We mean the very *idea* of place, of something so fundamental that it furnishes not only the basis for our sense of cities but also for our very perceptions of other things in general. There are two paths we could take at this point to provide the deeper insight necessary to appreciate the nature of place. One is to turn to the halls of modern science, searching through them for evidence that provides empirical testimony to the importance of place for humans and other living creatures. The other is to turn to the dusty manuscripts, but insightful views, of philosophers, scholars willing even to dispute the foundations of science. We take this latter course, believing that it can lead us to understand the deeper mysteries of the notion of place.

The first modern philosopher to take the notion of place seriously is Edward Casey. He has devoted a good deal of energy to explaining the meaning of place and how that meaning has changed over time. He also has helped to distinguish the concept of place from other key concepts, particularly those of space and time. And he has come to argue that while much of philosophy overlooked the significance of place, in favor of space, that place is as central to human existence as space and time.[6]

Casey maintains that in the course of the history of philosophy, the notion of place has somehow lost out to other concepts. Although the ancient Greeks, such as Aristotle, paid a great deal of attention to place, as philosophy developed over succeeding centuries the sense of place disappeared. In the writings of great minds like Gottfried Leibniz, for example, place disappears altogether and, in its stead, we find the notion of space, a notion that would become crucial both to later writings in philosophy as well as to discoveries in modern physics. The only allusion to place in the writings of Leibniz, Casey notes, is in his treatment of points in space, but such points are merely treated as sidelights, not the real material of interest. Space instead is the central concept for Leibniz. It comes to possess extension and magnitude. And one can further speak of it in precise mathematical terms, for which Leibniz proved to be the co-inventor of the calculus. But in his magnificent conception of space, there is no place for place.

Later philosophers would continue to treat place as a matter of minor, if not negligible importance. The great German philosopher, Immanuel Kant, who has left such a lasting mark on all later philosophy, treated time and space, for example, as basic intuitions of the "knowing subject." Kant regarded these intuitions as the media through which we know objects, both internal and external ones.[7] But, by themselves, they, in effect, represented nothing. They were elements without which we simply would know nothing. Place had no such important role to play in Kant's philosophical outlook. Yet he did not totally debunk place, as Casey notes. Kant, Casey observes, alluded to place through his invocation of the material body of the subject, a body that united both the intelligible and perceptual worlds.[8] Yet, apart from a brief discussion, Kant seems to have dismissed the idea of place altogether.

Nineteenth- and twentieth-century philosophers generally have not done much better in clarifying the nature of place. Or, rather, they did not do better until they began to grapple with the notion of ***body***. It is through their discussions of body, Casey advises us, that more recent philosophers have come to terms with the idea of place. Body, as a concept, has extension, as it does in the writings of Martin Heidegger, for example.[9] Body is something of which we are aware by the very nature of our basic perceptions. We sense, for instance, a difference between our left and our right, between the hand to our left and the hand to our right. These elements are not interchangeable. Hence, there must be something extensive and substantial about the nature of our body. Moreover, body not only has an extension in space, but it also has movement. If we can represent body, in space and time, we also find that body has movement: it goes back and forth, side to side, part of the natural extension of our different sides. So body has extension, and it has movement. And if it has both of these, then body must also occupy a position in space. And we can sense immediately that if it has position it must also have ***place***, for it could not have position without being in a place.

Casey provides an extremely deft and comprehensive handling of the way that place re-enters into philosophical discussions through analyses of the concept of body. Body, in effect, restores the notion of place to an important role in philosophy. And such a role is not of minor importance. Indeed, modern and post-modern philosophy makes much of the notion of body, using the concept as a way to speak of gender differences, between men and women. Such differences, to some philosophers, are so important as to provide entirely different orientations, of our senses and concepts, to whom we are, as palpable bodies, but also to whom others are.

There are other twentieth-century philosophers who provide some clues about the importance of place, though in a slightly different fashion. Hannah Arendt, one of the twentieth century's most insightful political philosophers, argues, for example, that the *polis*, or political community, represents a central kind of place for human beings.[10] The polis, she reminds us, is the embodiment of the political community for the ancient Greeks. It is the real site, the place, where the political community developed, through active discussion among its members about issues of public concern. And what is most important, to Arendt, about the concept of the polis is that it furnishes an open and public **place** where dialogue and engagement of citizens can occur. It is these features, so similar to the way we normally think of place, which stand out to Arendt as the defining elements of the polis.

MAJOR SOCIOLOGISTS ON PLACE: MARX, WEBER AND DURKHEIM

When we turn to consider the treatment of place by the major sociological thinkers – Karl Marx, Max Weber, and Emile Durkheim – we find a similar disregard as that among pre-twentieth century philosophers. In a way this should not be too surprising as these sociological thinkers were much influenced by other philosophers, such as Kant and Hegel who, themselves, paid scant attention to place. Yet our sociological forbears did provide a few clues in their writings to the significance of place.

Karl Marx

Karl Marx, the great nineteenth-century social theorist, was generally occupied with the comings and goings of social classes. Whatever added up to the nature of a social class, whatever contributed to the making of social history in time, were of the utmost importance to Marx. Indeed, as David Harvey has cogently argued, it was time, not space, and much less place that preoccupied Marx in his writings. History unfolded not so much in space, or on place, as it did over time. The revolutionary force of modern **capitalism**, though dispersed among different sites, was a force that unfolded not over space but over the course of time.[11]

Yet while Marx, himself, did not contribute substantially to an understanding of places, his longtime collaborator and friend, Friedrich Engels, did. Engels, in fact, wrote what many regard as one of the first great works of urban scholarship, *The Condition of the Working Class in England*.[12] Engels' father had manufacturing firms both in Bremen, Germany and Manchester, England. And in 1842 Engels went to live and work in Manchester. While there, he discovered how industrial capitalism had begun to transform not only society in general terms, as Marx and he had come to believe, but the very character of the newly-emergent industrial city. Manchester had grown into a major center whose work was concentrated in the production of textiles, materials that were shipped across the world, including to the Southern United States. When he returned home to Germany two years later, Engels wrote up his observations, developing as compelling and vivid a case against the injustices and tragedies of the new form of capitalism as had Charles Dickens.

Manchester

The book quickly became recognized as a classic, providing insight into the ways that the factory system, and the growing conflict between the wealthy and the working-class, unfolded. Engels described the different sections of Manchester, in particular, the filth and poverty of those forced to live in the working-class quarters compared to the relative comfort and ease of those who lived in the newer and more affluent areas. In vivid detail, Engels pictured the city, including even small maps of different quarters and streets, the living conditions of the population. His concerns for the working-class were evident in various passages, and his anger grew (as does that of the reader) through his vivid prose:

> But the most horrible spot . . . lies on the Manchester side (of the river). . . . In a rather deep hole in a curve of the Medlock and surrounded on all four sides by tall factories and high embankments, covered with buildings, stand two groups of about 200 cottages . . . in which live about 4,000 human beings, most of them Irish. The cottages are old, dirty, and of the smallest sort, the streets uneven, fallen into ruts and in part without drains or pavement; masses of refuse, offal, and sickening filth lie among standing pools in all directions; the atmosphere is poisoned by the effluvia from these, and laden and darkened by the smoke of a dozen tall factory chimneys. A horde of ragged women and children swarm about here, as filthy as the swine that thrive upon the garbage heaps and in the puddles.[14]

Engels' work thus helped to make concrete the more general claims and arguments of Marx, and of his indictment of capitalism. Moreover, it helped to reveal how the nature of the economic system could wreck havoc on the places where people lived, an insight that would continue to spawn countless important theoretical and empirical writings many decades afterwards.

Max Weber

Much like Marx, Max Weber seemed to sense little need for the notion of place in his writings. Weber was much more concerned with the elements and tendencies of modern social institutions, not only capitalism, like Marx, but, even more, the nature and growth of modern social organization, in the form of the modern bureaucratic organization. Weber does give somewhat more credibility to the fundamental notion of place in two writings, those on the city and the nature of the modern **state**.

In his work devoted exclusively to the nature of cities, ranging from those of ancient Greece to the city-states of the Middle Ages, Weber considers the wide array of cities that have existed.[14] He notes that they vary in form and type, from the predominantly political cities of the ancient Greeks and Romans to the commercially based cities of medieval Italy. They also vary in their physical construction, some having actual material barriers that enclose and separate them from the countryside, and in their social composition, some, like those of the Middle Ages, being sites identified with the ability of rural migrants to find new opportunities for themselves. But, underlying this diversity is a single insight – that the city is primarily a site where commerce and trade happen. It becomes **the physical location and representation** of the workings of the major economic institutions of the day. Weber writes, in particular, that the "'city' is a market-place (and the) local market forms the economic center of the colony in which . . . both the non-urban population and urbanites satisfy their wants for articles of trade and commerce."[15]

Nevertheless, over time, the city recedes in importance in Weber's reading of history, replaced by the emergence of the modern state. And this new institutional form, which begins to arise in the nineteenth and twentieth centuries, bears one striking parallel to that of the city, particularly to the city-states: it, too, is based upon a particular site or place. Weber observes that the defining characteristics of the modern nation-state are that it "exercises a legitimate monopoly over the means of violence" and that its legitimacy is bounded to a particular "territory."[16] In other words, like the city, the state is rich in institutions but such institutions are grounded, as it were, at a particular place.

Weber's discussions, while touching only incidentally on the nature of places, still leave us with an important sociological insight into the nature of place. In effect, whether in the older city-states or in the more recent nation-states, place is that location where the major institutions of a society do their visible and material work. In the city, one deals with the market place, while in the nation-state, we are dealing with the exercise of legitimate rule over a given **territory**. This insight is crucial for it commends us not merely to examine social institutions, in a general fashion, but to observe them in their concrete forms as they unfold over time in specific locations.[17]

Emile Durkheim

Emile Durkheim, the French sociologist who died early in the twentieth century, provides perhaps the most suggestive insights into the nature of place. Durkheim was concerned with understanding the very nature of the social order, seeing in this order a set of phenomena that were distinct from other realms, like that of biology. Social facts were of central interest to Durkheim, being collective ways of "seeing, thinking and acting" in the social world.[18] Society was a force that seemed, in some sense, to be invisible, but that left its mark on the world through its definition of objects and actions – things like social institutions such as the state, and actions like the rituals that are performed as part and parcel of religious activities.[19]

Based upon these presuppositions, then, Durkheim argues that there is an important distinction in the realm of social objects. People regard some objects with awe and power. Such objects would include specific religious symbols, like the cross among Christians, or the White House among American citizens. These sorts of objects, Durkheim notes, take on a **sacred** quality because of the awe they inspire within us. They are different from other sets of objects, those that we find in our everyday lives. The word-processors we use, the knives and forks we employ, the automobiles we drive, these and many other objects, being a part of our everyday lives, Durkheim claims, are by definition **profane**, or commonplace, objects.[20] Among Jews, to make the distinction perfectly clear, separate sets of dishes must be used at Passover, the springtime celebration of the Jews' exodus from the land of Egypt. Everyday dishes are set aside at this time, replaced by dishes that can only by used during the Passover meals and celebration. Passover dishes thus have a sacred place in Jewish belief; everyday dishes have only a profane, or commonplace, role.

So, too, it is with the notion of place for society. Some places, Durkheim observes, have a special and powerful presence for the members of society, much like Red Square for the Soviet Union. Durkheim writes of certain sites that take on awesome qualities, so endowed by their societies. Among the tribe of the Arunta, for example, these places are called the *ernatulunga*, and they are caves or caverns hidden away in isolated areas. They have been touched by the sacred elements of their societies, and they have become sanctuaries, a "place of peace . . . (or) a veritable asylum."[21] All other places have no such significance, precisely because they are commonplaces, those of everyday life. What lies behind the identification of that which is sacred, Durkheim would go on to argue, is the force of society. Thus, of course, whatever has the stamp of society, such as the laws governing places like cities or villages, must, in Durkheim's view, be regarded as bearing some semblance of the sacred. By contrast, whatever is my place, or your place, our own private places, in other words, pales by comparison with the power of the larger society to leave its imprint on place.

Summary

In sum, then, the concept of place has proven to be a rather minor concern to philosophers and sociologists, alike. There are hints, among both groups, of the importance of place, but no one thinker has truly taken on the notion as of seminal importance to our understanding of human nature. Nevertheless, as we have discovered in the nuanced treatments of philosopher Edward Casey, place is, indeed, a very important idea, one that reveals itself to us subtly through a sense of our own body and our body's extension in time and space. Like Casey we too believe that place is of central importance to human existence. And so we shall turn now to elaborate our own conception of it, drawing on some of the clues we have already uncovered.

A New Sociological Vision of Place

We believe that, in general, place occupies a central role in our lives as human beings. Just as consciousness seems to philosophers to be an important dimension of who we are, and just as language and communication furnish a means for establishing a sense of ourselves, so too place occupies a central role as we attempt to define who we are. It appears to be conventional wisdom that in our highly mobile world, place, as a property of our lives, has somehow disappeared from the scene, all but extinguished by our rapid comings-and-goings. But, indeed, no one, not even those road-weary travelers, find themselves in the absence of a need for place. It may be a hotel room, for overnight stays; or a business conference room, for important meetings; or a family home, to return to, at the end of a long business trip. There is, in short, a location, or a spot, where human activity occurs, of the most important and fundamental sort, and without which that which makes us human could not happen.

We believe further that there are certain natural and invariant connections that are associated with the nature of places (and human nature) for humans. Our sense of *placeness* only becomes meaningful through these connections. There are four of them: (1) a sense of individual identity, of who we are; (2) a sense of community, of being a part of a larger group, whether a family or a neighborhood; (3) a sense of a past and a future, of a place behind us and a place ahead of us; and (4) a sense of being at home, of being comfortable, of being, as it were, in place. Each of these meanings that attaches to the notion of place is, it appears to us, separate and distinct; yet all of them together probably overlay and reinforce one another.

Through these four points "sense of placeness is meaningful"

A SENSE OF PERSONAL IDENTITY

Human beings possess strong and intimate connections to the places in their lives. A stunning illustration of this quality appeared a few years back in an article published in *The New York Times*. It was written by Patricia Leigh and was about the house in which she had grown up in Highland Park, Illinois. She had learned that her old home was scheduled for demolition by its new owners and that, in its place, they planned to build a much larger contemporary structure, one on the order of 5,000 square feet. So attached did she feel to this house that she returned to Highland Park from her current residence on the East Coast, visiting the lot and the house. She also called another former resident of the house, Bill Bernstein, to tell him of its imminent destruction. Bernstein, like Leigh, was so connected to that house that he flew to Highland Park from Los Angeles, where he lived, and spent a night in the house, filming it with a video camera for his children and their children to see.

> "I wish I could have brought my kids, to let them know more of whom I am," he said recently. He was speaking for both his siblings and, unknowingly, my sisters and me. "You get to be our age, and you see the finish line," he continued. "I'm a big grown-up guy with kids now. But man, in my mind, I keep picturing that house." It was a fine house to grow up in, Leigh wrote, no more, no less. . . . Now it has entered the domain of memory. But a tiny part of us all will always be there, tucked away, in the chimney.[22]

Leigh and Bernstein, and others before and now others after them, shared a deep and intimate connection to that house on Sheridan Road in Highland Park. To those of us who never resided there, it might seem to have been merely a physical presence. But to Leigh and Bernstein it was a genuine piece of their lives.

All humans, regardless of where they may live and reside, experience a similar linkage between their own personal identity and the places they have lived. The universal sense of nostalgia, indeed, is based on a yearning to be in another place, one that has appropriate meaning and significance for individuals.[23]

A SENSE OF COMMUNITY

Just as individuals come to have a sense of themselves through their connections to places in their lives, so, too, social groups, ranging from families and friends to neighborhoods and communities, develop a powerful sense of affiliation and common identity based upon their connections to places. Neighborhoods, for instance, are not just connections among and between people, but they are communities of concern and relationship tied to specific sites and locales. Across the United States one can find countless illustrations of how such small communities form. In the city of Chicago, for example, sociologists have uncovered a number of these sites, so-called community areas. They are based upon a shared sense of identity among their members, and they are anchored in a specific locale, or place. Sociologist Gerald Suttles, in a famous study of different neighborhoods in Chicago, found that residents went to great lengths to defend and to identify with the areas where they lived.[24] These areas became for them ***territories*** – places in which they shared a common destiny, and which they went to great lengths to defend, creating boundaries that separated them from other neighborhoods.[25]

Sociologist Walter Firey also observes the important connections between the sense of place and that of community in his observations several decades ago in Boston. Firey found that certain sections of Boston became so significant to the life of the city that thoroughfares were actually routed around these areas. Such areas included not only the central Boston Common and Beacon Hill, but also certain cemeteries. Firey argues that even though it made perfect business sense to local planners and authorities to remove old cemeteries and to run roads directly through those lands, the areas themselves had become sacred representations of the community. Indeed, Firey drew upon the imagery of Durkheim, observing that "even more than the Common, the colonial burying grounds of Boston have become invested with a moral significance which renders them almost inviolable."[26] In death as in life, in other words, place takes on great significance.

Specific sites thus become marked by groups of people who reside in and on them as distinct sites of territory; place and common identity, or community, become inextricably intertwined, one with the other.

A SENSE OF A PAST AND A FUTURE

Though it may appear to be a paradox of sorts, given our modern emphasis on the reality of time, place also carries with it a strong sense of the past and the future. The sense of place, as it becomes visible to philosophers through a sense of the body, with extension and in space, provides the vehicle for understanding the past and the future of place. If we bear with us a body, which has movement, then it can move one way and another, to the side, but also to the back and to the front. Such movement does not merely suggest a past and a future, in temporal terms, but it also suggests that what is past is no longer the place of the present; and what is in the future is at another place, ahead of us.

Among the most telling illustrations of how places suggest both a past and a future people are those quotes and memories of immigrants to other lands. Immigrants typically possess a sense that by moving to a new land, a new place, they will find another place filled with greater promise than the one they have left. It is as though by abandoning their old residences they expect to find great riches and hopes in the new ones. A shift in place thus becomes not merely a shift from one site to another, but also a promissory note of endless new opportunities and hopes.

This sense of the past, as another place, then, is a sense that we have moved, bodily, from somewhere behind us and that we are moving forward. The past is, as our language suggests, behind us: it is away from us, in the distance. To think retrospectively, for example, is to think about the past, about something we have already experienced. When we are nostalgic for something, a memory, for example, it is something that is in the past. But it is not merely something we have left in time; it also is something we have left in place. We are no longer there, that place, that site and time, which stirs up our memories.

Likewise, and even more significantly for the lives of human beings, place strongly implies a future. "Tomorrow is another day," says Scarlett O'Hara in *Gone with the Wind*. But tomorrow is also another place. We can work harder tomorrow, but we can also find ourselves in a different, and perhaps, therefore, a better place, or position. When people die today, those who are young or who have been deathly ill, how often have we heard it said, "He is in a better place." So it is, with the nature of place and the sense of a future.

A SENSE OF BEING AT HOME

The last and final sense of place to which humans attach significance is the sense of being at home, and thus being comfortable, at peace, secure.[27] Such a sense complements and reinforces the other three human connections to place. It is conveyed best by that fundamental claim we sometimes make – "I feel out of place here." To feel out of place, of course, is to suggest that one is not at home and not comfortable where one is. Or obversely, to feel in place is to feel secure and to feel comfortable where one is. This is perhaps the most fundamental connection we human beings have to place, and why it is so surprising that place has been overlooked as philosophers turn their attention to the fundamental issues of human existence. Although our minds may roam freely across the universe, in an empty and sometimes occupied space, all of us, as living human beings, possess those sites in such space that help to locate us, and to ground us. They are our homes, our sites of comfort and of peace. They are the locales that placate us.

REVIEW

Human beings have significant attachments to places, we have argued. Such attachments represent, it seems to us, fundamental features of what it is to be human, and they exercise an influence over both our consciousness and our sentiments. They are significant in the sense that they seem to be intimately connected to what it means to be human; they fuel and fire one another; and over them are placed other meanings as well.

Place, we must emphasize, is a notion different from that of space with which it is sometimes conflated. Space is a medium independent of our existence in which there exist objects (including other human beings), objects that behave according to the basic laws of nature. Place is a unique and special location in that space notable for the fact that the regular activities of human beings occur there. Moreover, because it is a site of such activities, and all which they entail, it may furnish the basis for our sense of identity, as human beings, as well as for our sense of connection to other human beings, in other words, our sense of community. Place, in other words, is that special site, or sites, in space where people live and work, and where, therefore, they are likely to form intimate and enduring connections.[28]

Some may argue with our conception, suggesting that we may have reified the notion of place. But we insist that we have no more reified the notion of place than other philosophers have reified consciousness or being. Just as we take consciousness and being as part of our human nature, so, too, we take our sense of place, our place in the world. Moreover, just as our sense of place exercises a power over us and who we are, we also come to exercise a power over place as well. This is an important dialectic that is part and parcel of all experience, and especially of our experience in constructing places for us.

In addition, it is important to acknowledge that a long tradition in sociology, begun by the Chicago School of Sociology in the early part of the twentieth century, has taken place as important to an understanding of social behavior as we do (see chapter 2 below). But it made a fundamental error, or perhaps simply took the wrong turn on the matter. The error of the Chicago School was to seek linkages between the role of place for humans, and the role of place for animals and plants, hence the notion of *human ecology.*[29] Our view, in contrast, insists that place has a distinctive and unique role for human beings, their communities and cultures, one that is quite different than for other living things, and leads, therefore, to a whole set of different consequences than those identified by the Chicago School. This is not to deny nature a role in the places we occupy, but rather to argue that there are deep and profound differences between the settlements of humans and the settlements of other life forms.

We believe, further, that three important consequences follow immediately from this natural philosophy of place. The first is that forces, or agents, that disrupt our connections to place can foster a sense of deep distress felt strongly by people. Only the significance of these connections can possibly explain the vigorous reaction of many urban residents to attempts by real estate developers, or other groups, to invade their neighborhoods. And only their significance can explain why those immigrants who leave their communities and homes in old places attempt with great imagination to construct their elements in new places. Conversely, forces, or agents, that facilitate these attachments are thus encouraging something that is an intimate and natural part of our human nature. These connections, in other words, are felt as real. These consequences, of course, carry with them fundamental implications also for the design of real places, even places like cities, for their residents. Third, we may not always be aware of these connections; we may, in fact, be indifferent to them, an indifference that is fostered, in part, by the rapid pace of contemporary life. But such indifference should not be taken as evidence for the absence of the significance of place. Rather it is simply another layer of our modern world that intervenes between us and our connections to place, and thus another layer, as it were, that must be peeled away to discover the true underlying character of who we human beings really are.

Cities as Places

THE POWER OF SOCIAL INSTITUTIONS AND SOCIALLY IMPOSED MEANINGS IN THE MODERN METROPOLIS

Underlying the cities that we experience, then, is a fundamental sense and basic notion of place, of being in a somewhere at a sometime. In today's world, moreover, certain social agents and institutions play a major role in making their own definitions of urban places, and they do so through their exercise of great power. They construct the worldly – though, from our perspective, not the natural – meanings to urban places.

One of the principal social players in shaping the modern city is the local, or municipal, government. The role of local governments varies as between nations. In the United States, for example, the local government exercises its power to define and to dominate the life of the city in many unseen ways, ways that are not readily apparent to residents in their everyday lives. Those stoplights and stop signs, those roadways within the city, those parks and pedestrian boulevards, those public fountains and walkways, these and many more of the elements of the modern metropolis acquire their social and political definition – not their human definition – from the exercise of power by local government and its various branches. Where the government can exercise its authority over the local places, as in the United States, it does so, almost freely and almost always invisibly. Perhaps the greatest authority to be exercised by local government is in the definition of the boundaries between the city and those places outside it. These definitions are of vital importance, not only signaling those members who are inside and those who are outside the city, but also the limits to the authority of local government.

A range of other laws is put into effect as well by local governments, including zoning ordinances that define what can go where within the local area. Moreover, as we shall discover later in this book, local property taxes also furnish the funds for many municipal activities in the United States, ranging from the work of police departments to that of schools. This means, in effect, that where a locality contains many rich residents, it will be able to provide for a far better range of local services, such as schools, than where it does not. The implications of this feature of local government in the United States are thus very far-reaching.

(2) A second major player is that of the national, or federal, government. In countries like Great Britain, or Canada, the national government plays a much more prominent role in setting definitions and laws than in the United States. And yet, even in the United States, the federal government has come to play an ever more significant role, especially over the course of the last half of the twentieth century. The massive housing developments that began in the late 1930s, accelerating after the end of World War II, were the work of the federal government and its officials, for example. Pursued with the best of intentions, in fact, like so many other social products, they have had serious unintended consequences. Critics note that such developments have promoted high crime rates, and led to trafficking in drugs and other forms of criminal activity. Thus, just as the federal government was able to construct, it also was able to deconstruct them, beginning in the late 1990s. The plan now was to build smaller housing developments, and to encourage a mix of low- and high-income residents. Such housing developments are only one illustration of the vast power of the federal government to exercise its authority over the modern urban environment in America.

(3) Private developers and their agents as well as financiers represent a third major force in the contemporary world for setting the definition and the tone for the modern metropolis and for smaller settings as well. There are national developers whose work is evident in a variety of different cities. They include such figures as Samuel Zell, a Chicago-based real estate entrepreneur who has vast holdings and developments across the United States. There are also local developers who create new housing and commercial developments in various cities. In New York City, for example, Donald Trump and his firm stand out as one prime example. In other countries, such as Great Britain, there are also the special firms that have built great housing and commercial properties, among them the massive and controversial Canary Wharf development in London. Canary Wharf was begun by Canadian financiers and developers along the River Thames, and has become the site of a finan-

cial district that rivals the historic financial center in London.

More and more, these great developers have played a significant part in helping to redefine the nature of the urban place. Many times their works turn out to be important and to foster the building of community among residents. The first of the great housing developers at the end of World War II was William Leavitt. He created the massive development that became known as Levittown on Long Island, New York. Constructed of housing that was identical from lot to lot, and street-to-street, Levittown was the first great experiment of new suburban housing. Studies by sociologists showed that such suburban developments had both their strengths and weaknesses: they did help to promote community among residents, but the communities they fashioned often lacked the diversity by race and income-level so characteristic of the United States.[30] More recently, developers have had a hand in fashioning new cities, ones that become characterized by their over-arching themes, and a process that some sociologists refer to as the "Disneyfication" of America.[31]

 The last great force to play a major role in today's urban environment is that of local residents themselves, by no means insignificant players. Residents, as a collection of families and friends, appear to possess far less power to leave their imprint on the contemporary urban landscape than do the large political and business corporations that dominate the life of the city. But almost everywhere residents make an effort to create for themselves a place in their own image, to which they can feel securely attached. The sense of neighborhood that downtown residents create is very important, as it is throughout the metropolitan area. In the suburban districts of large cities, both the older middle-class suburbs and the newer, more diverse working class ones, neighbors work to develop a strong (and natural) sense of community among themselves. There often is an easy give-and-take to life in the suburbs that is not to be found in the large public housing projects of central cities. Although each neighborhood is likely to be somewhat distinct, and often to involve its own particular set of issues, there are concerns that transcend individual neighborhoods, and the lives of separate residents. Acknowledging this, in the 1970s and 1980s, especially, national organizations emerged in the United States to work on problems common to many neighborhoods and their residents.

The modern metropolis, in sum, bears the material and symbolic imprint of several different major groups and social institutions. Different meanings and definitions come to be fashioned and attached to the real places of the city, as of the suburb and the neighborhood, as these players contest among themselves for political supremacy and dominance. Although the local government (or in other nations, often the national government) and the real estate community play perhaps the most powerful roles in leaving their mark, creating new zoning laws or new housing projects, many residents work hard to sustain and to continue their own natural and vital connections to place. Over the course of the 1970s and 1980s especially, large numbers of neighborhood associations appeared throughout American cities, for example, testimony to the courage and attachment to place of local residents.

The various actors and players in today's cities figure importantly into the nature and definition of cities as places. Institutions, like the local government, help to define the very nature of these places through a variety of laws and statutes. To the degree that these other definitions facilitate or encourage our natural connections to place, we would argue, they work in harmony with our tendencies, as humans. But to the extent that they work in opposition to these connections, such as that of our own personal identity or sense of community, they work against our own natural inclinations. Our neighbors and residential groups obviously come closest to working our own behalf, seeking to secure our natural connections, to foster the identity we have with places, to encourage a sense of community, to make us feel at home in places. Other forces, such as private developers, may work against such natural connections, though such opposition is not to be automatically assumed. Growing numbers of developers, through their work to create such new things as "sustainable communities," can help to secure our natural connections to places. Local governments, which often seem to be opposed to the work of neighbors and residential groups, also can help to facilitate our natural connections to places. They may do so through generous efforts to create public places for common enjoyment, such as parks and other recreational areas.

But most often the major institutions of urban places seem to work in opposition to our own efforts to make such places into the natural expression for our human connections. One major line of division, and opposition, occurs between residents, neighbors and private developers. In many modern cities, including many in the rapidly growing areas of the South and Southwest, there are constant and continuing battles between these two sides, producing heated confrontations in front of various city councils or other branches of local government. In some places, like Santa Barbara, California, the citizens have been sufficiently effective to produce a quid pro quo from the private developers, securing in exchange for new developments the creation of public park lands. In other places, the developers have been compelled to help to create certain amounts of mixed-income housing.

The net result of these events has been to produce in many cities a fragmented and contentious metropolis, one that is far from what our human ideal might recommend. It is a contested metropolis, with battles not only occurring between local residents and developers, but also over the very natural connections that people have to places. The modern metropolis, whether in the United States or in France, has become something of a layered mosaic of alternative definitions and meanings, some of which, like those of residential groups, help to foster our natural connections, but others of which work in opposition to them.

CITIES AND EVERYDAY SOCIAL LIFE

It is in the very character of our human nature, we believe, that cities, as places, and everyday life go together hand-in-hand. Everyday life in urban areas is filled with noises and people. And it is those very qualities that help to furnish the sense of identity and social connection that intimately connect human beings to the places where they reside. Social observers have done much in recent years to reveal how the sense of place emerges in the course of everyday life on city streets and sidewalks.

William H. Whyte, for instance, wrote a wonderful book on the everyday traffic in cities, and he did so by observing the everyday life on the streets and sidewalks of many different cities, but especially New York City where he lived.[32] His chapters, on the social life of the streets, and street people, convey the richness of urban life that connects people to these places. He writes, for instance, of the process of "schmoozing," the social intercourse on the streets of cities, noting that it occurs all over city streets. People mill and walk about on mild days in the city, some "groups, as on Seventh Avenue, are of the semipermanent floating kind, and many last the whole hour."[33] These activities, plus many more, provide easily accessible testimony to the strong and intimate bonds that occur during the course of daily life in the city.

Perhaps the person to most elevate the importance of the city and everyday life in contemporary thought is the social critic, author and observer, Jane Jacobs. In her seminal work on the city, *The Death and Life of Great American Cities*, Jacobs argued against the prevailing tendencies in the 1950s to isolate people from the traffic on city sidewalks and businesses.[34] Instead, she argues, cities, as real places, must seek to create an intimate mix of people with one another: that is the very nature, she said. There must be noise and congestion; there must be a regular pattern of social intercourse that takes place on the urban arcades. It is only through such constant commingling of people, one with another, that the life of cities actually transpires. We, of course, believe that the realities Jacobs sought to create are qualities that actually serve to facilitate and to foster our own natural connections to places.

More recently, key sociologists have written precisely about the nature of everyday life and the course of social life in the city. In the award-winning book, *Streetwise*, sociologist Elijah Anderson speaks about the nature of life in the black and white sections of central Philadelphia. In a work filled with important and surprising observations, Anderson writes of the nature of life not only within specifically black and white areas, but also how boundaries form between them.

> Informal boundaries are consummated through the routes people take in meeting an average day's basic needs and desires. The newsstand where one buys the Sunday paper, the store one runs to for a quart of milk, and the streets one travels to visit a friend express one's sense of the boundaries . . . Through such experiences, one learns where one can and cannot go without receiving an unfavorable reaction. Thus whites tend not to stray into Northon (the black area), and young black men and women may think carefully before walking through the streets of the Village (the white area) at certain times of day and night.[35]

Thus, to Anderson the nature of everyday life in cities partly encourages, but partly discourages, social intercourse among people: our natural connections to community are encouraged within racial areas, but deeply discouraged across their informal boundaries.

Everywhere, not only in American cities, we can observe much of this daily traffic. It is a natural and important part of the lives of residents and the cities in which they live. Whether it is in downtown Tokyo, or in central London, people are engaged in daily activities on metropolitan streets. Some places, like London, strongly encourage such traffic, through a prominent and rich assortment of almost village-like markets. Even places in the United States have sought to restore an atmosphere of civility and social life through their creation of new markets and streets along which neighbors and strangers can meet and shop.

Some of the most interesting, yet least noticed activity of the modern metropolis occurs as homeless people create their own places on the streets and sidewalks of the city. Just as we encounter markets, so too we encounter many of the homeless, numbers of whom have been created through a variety of means and sources. In a recent work, sociologist Mitchell Duneier (1999) has written of these everyday residents on the streets and sidewalks of the city. They create their own sense of "habitat," he observes in a careful and meticulous accounting of their activity. "Perhaps the most of the basic elements of this habitat," Duneier writes, is a density of pedestrians . . . Another characteristic of the habitat is the availability of cheap or free food . . . (And yet a) third characteristic of the habitat is an abundance of public places to sleep with little impunity."[36]

The homeless, those men and women who appear at first sight to be placeless, ironically may provide the most telling and powerful lessons about cities as places. Their activities, designed to find comfort in the seeming cold indifference of urban thoroughfares, reveal once more how natural and important our connections are to the places in which we live. Homeless men and women may lack the shelter most of the rest of us have. But what they lack in buildings, they consciously fashion for themselves, as they organize and establish their own sense of identity and community in the seemingly indifferent places of the modern metropolis.

THE MOBILITY OF CAPITAL AND LABOR, AND THEIR IMPACT ON CITIES

Among the most powerful forces that now intrude on the nature of urban life, in America and elsewhere, are those of modern capital and labor, business firms and workers. These forces have begun to remake not only the nature of the world's economy, but have also left their own mark on the modern metropolis.

In part, the new economic and political forces are doing so by reshaping the nature of the local economies, and the nature of the local societies and social classes. The question we must consider is this: how has the new mobility of capital and labor – the new immigrants, the international companies that have moved into cities – left its impact both in real terms on places, and in our own natural connections to places? There are several obvious consequences of these changes. For one thing, the new immigrants have established new small enclaves throughout many larger urban centers, enclaves that provide yet another way and form in which humans seek to connect to places. Many such **enclaves** re-create the prior residences of the immigrants. In effect, they transport with them their communities from abroad, and reconnect to the new places. In so doing, they have left important new imprints on the nature of their new cities, both visually and in their impact on the local economies. For another thing, the new international business players that enter the urban arena provide yet another force for remaking cities, often against the wishes of local residents. While such outside firms bring in new capital, providing both new jobs and other new investments, they also add a new distinctive layer to reshaping the nature of the modern metropolis. In some sites, such as China, these new players have been welcomed in with open arms, actually creating entirely new cities in their wake.

Finally, the new mobility of capital and labor adds a certain new richness to the life of the metropolitan area. They add to the ethnic and national diversity of the metropolis, both in the form of new ethnic enclaves and in the everyday traffic on the streets of the city. Visually and culturally they have helped to create a new and powerful display of the modern urban places. It remains to be seen whether, for new immigrants, for example, the enclaves that they have created will have a broader and important impact on the lives of native residents. Will they help, for instance, to spread and thus to encourage our natural connections to places, as immigrants have done in the past, or will they simply so add to the pace of modern life that they disrupt these connections? One can only hope that these forces, which have been unleashed over the course of the past two decades, will help to make the real modern metropolis into one that more closely resembles our ideals.

BUILDINGS AND CITIES

Let us conclude this brief overview of the major elements of the modern city by considering buildings, or what is called the "**built environment**," and those who design and build them. Apart from real estate brokers and private developers, no single group of people has exercised as much control over the nature of places as architects. They are the men and women, after all, whose job it is to construct actual places so that they will be attractive to their residents. And many have done so with great flair, establishing towering structures that both house people and define the skyline of the modern city. It was architects and their allies, certain city planners, who seemed to have fashioned places that so infuriated and drew out the wrath of Jane Jacobs in the 1950s. Nevertheless, various architects have left important signature works that help to define the urban landscape. Mies Van der Rohe, in the 1930s through the 1950s, created fashionable buildings on the Outer Drive of Chicago, for instance. Frank Lloyd Wright's creation of Monona Terrace in Madison, Wisconsin, a project that took more than half a century to complete, helped to bring new attention to that state capitol. And Frank Gehry's wonderful piece of architecture, the Guggenheim Museum in Bilbao, Spain, has not only revived the tourist life of Bilbao, but it has taught us, once again, how important pieces of architecture can be in symbolizing the significance and character of particular urban places. Architects, in the hope that such designs would create monuments that defined and identified the singularity of an urban place, have designed all of these creative works.

City planning is a relatively new profession. It got its informal start late in the nineteenth century in England. Certain figures, such as the Englishman, Patrick Geddes, left an important mark on the history of city planning, providing designs and ambitions for creating new and effective towns and villages. Others, like Ebenezeer Howard, also contributed to our visions of new cities. Howard, in particular, drew up large and careful designs of relatively small villages, hoping to create some useful balance between local businesses, residential areas, and green belts and parklands. Such designs as these have contributed greatly to the efforts by today's city planners to try to create urban places that would be meaningful and attractive places for people to live. Yet many times their efforts have gone awry, falling under the influence and hegemony of private developers and local capitalists.

Nonetheless, today there are even newer and more sophisticated urban visions being created. Among the most interesting are those of planners who wish to create "sustainable communities," localities that provide not only a comfortable setting for residents, but also work to create a more effective harmony between the constructions of man, and the work of nature. These are visions that seek to bridge the social with the ecological, the basic requirements of human beings with the demands of the broader natural environment.

Let us conclude this opening chapter with the pieces of one such vision, one that helps to articulate our own sense of the importance of place, in the broadest terms, for the settlements of men and women: "To foster a sense of place, communities must nurture built environment and settlement patterns that are uplifting, inspirational and memorable, and that engender a special feeling of attachment and belonging . . . [In] a sustainable [community], [every] effort is made to create and preserve places, rituals, and events that foster greater attachment to the social fabric of the community."[37]

Such an ideal community would make real the connections to place that are part and parcel of which we all are.

Notes

We are very grateful to Isaac Balbus, Judith Friedman, Kevin Fox Gotham, and Harvey Molotch for their comments on an earlier draft of this chapter.

1   As quoted in Edward S. Casey, *The Fate of Place* (Berkeley: University of California Press, 1997), p. 4.

2   Edward Relph, *Place and Placelessness* (London: Pion, 1976), p. 43.

3   Also see Kevin Fitzpatrick and Mark LaGory, *Unhealthy Places: The Ecology of Risk in the Urban Landscape* (New York: Routledge, 2000); and Sharon Zukin, *Landscapes of Power* (Berkeley: University of California Press, 1991). It must be noted that Zukin uses place in a somewhat different fashion than we do, namely, to refer to the permanence of social institutions.

4   Besides the other books mentioned here, also see John Brinckerhoff Jackson, *A Sense of Place, a Sense of Time* (New Haven, Connecticut: Yale University Press, 1994), and the excellent discussion in Dolores Hayden, *The Power of Place: Urban Landscapes as Public History* (Cambridge, Mass.: The MIT Press, 1995).

5   Kathleen S. Crittenden and Kelvin S. Rodolfo, "Bacolor Town and Pinatubo Volcano: Coping with Recurrent Lahar Disaster," pp. 43–65 in John Grattan and Robin Torrence, eds., *Natural Diasters, Catastrophism, and Cultural Change*. One World Archaeology Series (London: Routledge, 2000). Our great thanks to Professor Crittenden for her willingness to share her research and insights with us for this particular chapter.

6   Casey, *The Fate of Place*; and Edward S. Casey, *Getting Back into Place: Toward a Renewed Understanding of the Place-World* (Bloomington, Indiana: Indiana University Press, 1993).

7   Immanuel Kant, *The Critique of Pure Reason.*

8   Casey, *The Fate of Place.*

9   Martin Heidegger, *Being and Time.*

10   Hannah Arendt, *The Human Condition* (Chicago: the University of Chicago Press, 1958).

11   David Harvey, *The Condition of Postmodernity.* (Oxford: Blackwell Publishers, 1990); Edward W. Soja, *Postmodern Geographies* (London: Verso, 1989).

12   Friedrich Engels, *The Condition of the Working Class in England.* Edited with an Introduction and Notes by David Mclellan. Originally published in 1844 (Oxford: Oxford University Press, 1993, 1999).

13   Ibid., p. 72.

14   Max Weber, *The City.* Translated and edited by Don Martindale and Gertrud Neuwirth (New York: The Free Press, 1958).

15   Ibid., p. 67.

16   Max Weber, "Politics as a Vocation," pp. 77–128 in C. Wright Mills and Hans Gerth, eds., *From Max Weber: Essays in Sociology and Social Psychology* (New York: Oxford University Press, 1958).

17   See also Gerald D. Suttles, *The Social Construction of Communities* (Chicago: the University of Chicago Press, 1972), esp. Part III, on Territory.

18   Emile Durkheim, *The Rules of the Sociological Method.*

19   Emile Durkheim, *The Elementary Forms of the Religious Life.* Translated from the French by Joseph Ward Swain (New York: Collier Books, 1961).

20   Ibid.

21   Ibid., p. 142.

22   *The New York Times,* B1, November 14, 1996.

23   Relph, *Place and Placelessness.*

24   Suttles, *The Social Order of the Slum: Ethnicity and Territory in the Inner City* (Chicago: University of Chicago Press, 1968).

25   Suttles, *The Social Construction of Communities.*

26   Walter Firey, "Sentiment and Symbolism as Ecological Variables," *American Sociological Review,* 10 (April 1945); pp. 140–8.

27   Relph, *Place and Placelessness.*

28   We are very grateful to Isaac Balbus for bringing this point to light, and also for his very useful references to other writings on place, especially that of Relph.

29   Our criticism here of the Chicago School is not intended to continue the almost savage attacks against this group of sociologists, attacks that began in the early 1970s (see chapter 2 below). But their paradigm did for a long while represent the dominant approach in sociology, and our brief remarks here about their approach simply acknowledge the tremendous impact they have had upon the way we think today, as sociologists, about urban areas.

30   In recent years there has been a growing diversity of suburbs in terms of their racial and ethnic features. Some of this diversity is the product of the post-1965 immigration to the United States; some of it is simply the result of new working-class suburbs. For data on such diversity see Richard Harris and Peter Larkham, editors, *Changing Suburbs. Foundation, Form and Function* (London: E and FN Spon and New York: Routledge, 1999); and Richard Alba, John Logan, Brian Stults, Gilbert Marzan, and Wenquan Zhang, "Immigrant Groups in the Suburbs: A

Reexamination of Suburbanization and Spatial Assimilation," *American Sociological Review*, 64, 3 (June 1999): 446–60.

31 Mark Gottdiener, Claudia C. Collins, and David R. Dickens, *Las Vegas: The Social Production of an All-American City* (Oxford: Blackwell Publishers, 1999); and Zukin, *Landscapes of Power*.

32 William H. Whyte, *The City: Rediscovering the Center* (New York: Doubleday, 1988).

33 Ibid, p. 16.

34 Jane Jacobs, *The Death and Life of Great American Cities* (New York: Random House, 1961).

35 Elijah Anderson, *Streetwise: Race, Class, and Change in an Urban Community* (Chicago: the University of Chicago Press, 1990), pp. 46–7.

36 Mitchell Duneier, *Sidewalk* (New York: Farrar, Straus and Giroux, 1999), pp. 144–5.

37 Timothy Beatley and Kristy Manning, *The Ecology of Place: Planning for Environment, Economy and Community* (Washington, D.C.: Island Press, 1997), p. 32.

Social Theory and the City

We have argued that cities, as places, are very important to our lives as human beings. They provide an anchor to our existence, and thus leave an important impact on our lives. Every urban social scientist would, in all likelihood, agree with the main lines of our argument. Yet there are wide-ranging differences among them when it comes to the elements that we should employ in explaining and exploring the nature of cities. Some of these differences can be traced to the early foundations of sociological thought. Writers on the city who have been influenced by Karl Marx, for example, are likely to view it one way, whereas those who have been influenced by Emile Durkheim are apt to think of it in a very different manner.

Here in this chapter we want to introduce you to the basic outlines of these different perspectives. We believe it is important in a foundational book, such as this, that you learn of the alternative points of view about urban life. We will cast our net widely in discussing theories, bringing in the writings of some figures who, by profession, are geographers but whose works bear directly on our concerns as social scientists to penetrate the meaning of cities. Moreover, to help you appreciate the alternative arguments, we also shall discuss their various strengths and weaknesses, thus allowing you to compare them to one another. In particular, we shall consider each of the following perspectives: (1) human ecology; (2) neo-Marxist; (3) the growth machine; (4) cultural perspectives; (5) historical/institutional; and finally (6) global perspectives.

Human Ecology: Of Populations and People

In the study of sociology we generally are introduced to its beginnings far
from American shores, in Europe, and in the writings of figures like Karl Marx
and Max Weber. But sociology also had special beginnings in the United
States, ones that would play a great role in the development of an urban
sociology. Early in the twentieth century, a group of scholars worked together
at the University of Chicago. In the course of doing so they created a particular brand of sociology that was very different from that in European univer-
sities. The University of Chicago had one of the first sociology departments in
the United States, established under the leadership of Albion Small in the
1890s. Two decades later, the department had become home to several important sociologists, including Robert Park, Ernest Burgess, Louis Wirth, and
W. I. Thomas.[1]

Park exercised perhaps the greatest influence over the intellectual shape
of the Department. Trained in Germany, he was influenced by the writings
of several European scholars, especially Georg Simmel and several students
of the field of ecology.[2] Park creatively combined these influences and di-
rected his interests, and that of his students, to undertaking work on his immediate locale, that of the city of Chicago. Whereas the great European social
theorists cut their teeth by examining the major waves and groups in history, like those of the growing ranks of capitalists and the working-classes,
Park and his associates turned their attention to more immediate objects.
They developed what became known as a sociology of the city, and of all
manner and form in the city. Eventually they created a rich catalog of studies of the city. Such studies provided information about how space was used
in the city as well as about the growing numbers of new people who were
arriving on American shores from Europe.[3]

The scholars of the Chicago School took the notion of place very seriously,
helping to fashion the first arguments on behalf of the ways that human beings become attached to and refashion their places within the city. While
Europeans were examining the formation of social classes, or the emerging
nature of factories and work across the nations of Europe, Park, Burgess and
Wirth were examining the city of Chicago and its new residents. They created a rich panoramic portrait of the city, one that took in all regions of the
city, from its interior to its fringes, from the downtown to the residential areas. Thus, it was not surprising that eventually one of the chief criticisms
that would emerge about the University of Chicago sociology program was
that it was based exclusively in Chicago.[4]

Park's program was guided by concepts and ideas that he had picked up
during his studies in Europe. Rather than looking at the new immigrants
from Europe, for example, as clusters of people who were trying to make their

way in a new land, Park and his colleagues thought of them as new ***population groups***. And rather than thinking of the city of Chicago simply as a city, full of its all-too-obvious noise and clatter, and of the direct and new buildings, Park imagined it to be a new **environment.** Thus he created a way of seeing all that around him in terms of how new population groups, i.e. the immigrants, entered and adapted to their new environment, i.e. the city of Chicago.[5]

This view turned into what today we call a paradigm.[6] It became a broad theoretical perspective, not only on the city, but also on social life, more generally. It drew its inspiration from writings in biology and ecology, writings that sought to connect the patterns of life of all living things to their broader material environments. It conceived important connections between the ways that human beings in the city made their settlements with the ways that animals sought to find a niche and home on plains and prairies. Just as plants, for example, had to adapt to their surroundings, of other plants, so, too, the perspective fashioned by Park and his colleagues posited that humans, in order to make their way in the city, had to adapt to other human beings as well as to the social institutions found in the city.

Human ecology was the name by which this perspective would eventually become known.[7] It saw the unfolding and development of urban life as parallel in many ways to the unfolding and development of life, in general. It developed and even imported concepts that originally were used to speak about the patterns of life, and contest, among plants and animals. Human beings, to the human ecologists, competed over the use of land and territory, just as plants and animals did. One group succeeded another group in a particular place in the city, just as one group of animals might succeed another on some plains. **Competition** and **succession**, of human beings, became conceptual staples for the studies by human ecologists.[8]

When thus applied to studies of the city of Chicago, the human ecology perspective took note of the particular and specific places where people settled, and of the differences between the places of work and of residence in the city. The view also maintained that there were vital and important differences between the central and the outer parts of cities. The competition for land, for example, was at its most extreme in the center of the city for this was the site of greatest influence over the rest of the city. It was here that the dominant social institutions were located – the newspapers, the railroad stations, the offices of the city government. All power and influence over the life of the city was, in effect, centralized. And because of this, among other things, the price for land was at its highest in the center of the city. This was why only the most wealthy firms and industries were located in the center – why it was in the center of the city that the financial district was to be found as well.

But human ecology was not just about the stable patterns of life and location in the city of Chicago. It also was about change and movement in the city, so much a part of the life of real cities. Certain tendencies and trends became uncovered through the work of the human ecologists. Thus, for example, it appeared from their early work that immigrants, while settling first on some of the outer boundaries of the center of the city, eventually would move to a city's outskirts. This was certainly true for the children, and grandchildren, of the original immigrants. In addition, it also appeared to be true

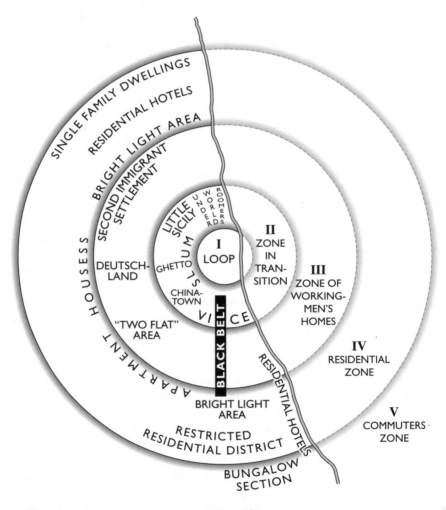

Figure 2.1   Concentric zone portrait of Chicago[9]
Source: Robert E. Park and Ernest W. Burgess, *The City*. Copyright © 1925 by the University of Chicago Press. Chicago, Illinois. The figure comes from: Ernest W. Burgess, "The Growth of the City: An Introduction to a Research Project," pp. 47–62. Chart II, page 55.

that there was a strong tendency for businesses to settle in the center of the city, while residences tended to grow up on the outskirts. These general changes, and patterns of settlement, all became frozen in time and space through what has become perhaps the most celebrated portrait and legacy of the Chicago school, Ernest Burgess's portrait of the city of Chicago early in the twentieth century.

A host of details about the social life and characteristics of the residents of the city would eventually become filled in by the students of Park, Burgess and Wirth. Seminal writings were done of particular classes and types of people living in the city, including hustlers and criminals.[10] The underside of urban life was of great interest to the Chicago school of sociology. In addition, there were features of urban life, beyond the scope of the human ecological paradigm, that were embraced by some of the scholars. Louis Wirth penned another classic product, a brief and general analysis of the tendencies of urban life in modern America.[11] Wirth, drawing on the inspiration of Simmel, argued that urban life at the turn of the century lent itself to a kind of impersonality and rapid pace that was distinctly different from life in rural areas. Money became the medium of exchange, a form so impersonal and so impartial that it would come to embody and to further the anonymity of life in the city.[12] While most Chicago human ecologists focused their attention on a single or individual city, Robert McKenzie put forth a systemic view by suggesting that cities could form a hierarchy based on their functional dominance and linkages.[13]

Well into the twentieth century, the ideas and arguments of the human ecologists remained the most compelling and influential of all perspectives on the city. At mid-century, Amos Hawley, a sociologist at the University of Michigan, strengthened the program of the human ecologists by fashioning a major theory of the city.[14] He transformed what had been a grab bag of insights and perceptions into a full-fledged theory about the nature of the city. He wrote of the city as a mechanism for the adaptation of human beings to life in a larger environment. He spoke of the nature of dominance in the city, and how certain institutions came to dominate others because they were more important, in general, to the process of adaptation. And he pursued the idea of interdependence of the various groups and institutions of the city, noting how such interdependence was a key element to the survival of the human community in cities.

Eventually the legacy of the human ecologists came to include a range of ideas and concepts, from adaptation to population groups, from urban transportation to voluntary associations that guided the work of many urban students.[15] But it also was scholarship whose energy and life span could only extend so far. And by the latter half of the twentieth century its dominance in the field of urban sociology would be challenged by other views.

The greatest strength perhaps of the school of human ecology was that it had invented such a strong and systematic way of looking at the world, particularly the world of cities and human beings. Grounded in writings of biologists and ecologists, it had an appeal based, in part, on its concerns and linkages to other views about the origins of human life. Moreover, it had exploited the advantages of being housed at a university in one of the great cities of America, and thus could send an endless number of students into nearby settings in search of the next empirical discovery.

But there were evident problems as well. As many scholars later would note, there was a danger in rooting a scientific view of the city mainly on research located in just one city. The concentric pattern of settlement and business uncovered by Burgess and his students, for example, later was found not to describe a number of other cities in the world. Moreover, by transferring certain basic ideas and concepts directly from the work of ecologists into the realm of human settlements, the human ecologists seemed to have bypassed certain important questions. Were human settlements really comparable to those of plants and animals? How could one compare the complexity of social institutions, like that of business firms or government, with the patterns of life emergent among colonies of ants? And what role did consciousness, and culture, play in human life in the city?[16]

Questions such as these led eventually to deep and searching revisions of the human ecological paradigm. And in the process, they also led to some fundamental leaps into other realms of theory.

Neo-Marxist Writings: From Place to Space

In the time since the late 1960s the figure to exercise the greatest influence over the study of cities is Karl Marx, the great social theorist. In a way this is rather peculiar because Marx wrote virtually nothing about cities, per se. As we suggested in chapter 1, however, his lifelong collaborator, Friedrich Engels, did write a particularly compelling and fascinating account of nineteenth-century Manchester, England. But while Engels managed to portray the deep and powerful ways in which class inequalities made themselves manifest on the urban landscape, most of his energies, and those of Marx, were devoted to explaining the nature of modern capitalism and laying the foundations for Communism among the growing working classes of the world.

In the twentieth century, a number of writers have stretched and extended the ideas of Marx, showing how they can now be applied to understand the development of the modern metropolis. Here we shall discuss some of the key ideas of the leading urban interpreters of Marx: Henri Lefebvre, Manuel Castells, and David Harvey.

Henri Lefebvre

The Marxist writer who has exercised the greatest influence over the study of cities, including the work both of Manuel Castells and David Harvey, is the French sociologist, Henri Lefebvre. It is only in recent years, with the translation of his writings into English, that the novelty of his work has become known to the English-speaking world. His main contribution has been to single out the realm of **space**, and to explore the ways in which it becomes implicated in the creation and development of urban areas.[17] In a sense he moved the analysis and discussion of cities away from the notion of place, which had been one of the strongest contributions of the Chicago School, to the concept of space, thus linking the dynamics of cities to the more general concern of philosophers with the ideas both of space and of time.

The challenge to the creation of a strong and powerful urban analysis among Marxists is that Marx not only failed to develop a program for the study of cities, but that his work was grounded in two major themes: the influence of the economy on social life, and the significance of time in the origins and development of humankind. Marx took on the ideas of David Ricardo and Adam Smith, which furnished the basic building-blocks for the study of economic life, and used them to reveal the inconsistencies and contradictions in the manner in which the economy operated. The "invisible hand," to which Smith referred in arguing on behalf of his insight that the purposeful work of individuals ultimately contributed to the progress and well-being was, to Marx's way of thinking, nothing but an illusion. Modern capitalism worked because the ideas of the capitalists had taken root and become the structural basis for the way that people worked, and lived, under capitalism. The state, among other institutions, worked to maintain the rule of the capitalists by furnishing the necessary political power to uphold capitalists when their rule, or individual decisions, might be challenged. So, too, the theory of value proposed by David Ricardo, the theory that said that products achieved their value by virtue of the labor invested in them, was viewed by Marx also as an illusion. Workers endowed their products with value but, according to Marx, in the process they unwittingly provided a surplus to the capitalists who owned those products, and thus the very basis for the growth and development of capitalism.

Yet these inconsistencies and difficulties with the working of capitalism, Marx believed, only became apparent over the course of time and history. Time became the medium through the forces of capitalism unfolded and developed. Events and practices that happened in the past came to shape decisively the actions of humans and social classes at present and well into the future. The famous quotation attributed to Marx, that "(m)en make their own history, but they do not make it just as they please; they do not make it under circumstances chosen by themselves, but under circumstances directly found, given and transmitted from the past" means precisely this – that key events and decisions of the past create structures and dictate decisions that we make at present.[18] The original accumulation of capital, for example, through the agricultural surplus developed in rural areas was a decisive event in the creation of modern capitalism, furnishing the template by which the surplus laborers would be appropriated by capitalists to develop their great industrial engine. The past, in general, weighed heavily on the actions of humankind, so heavily that it was only through the decisive events of a revolutionary transformation (the *Aufhebung* first conceptualized by G. W. F. Hegel) that humankind was able to break free of the fetters of the past. Revolution (and transformation), was action that not only required the practical work of humans but was impossible outside of the framework of time and history.

But what about space, the other central icon of thinking promoted through the work of philosophers dating back to Aristotle? Marx said nothing about space. And this was the challenge that Lefebvre took up – how to think about space and to do so, more or less, as a rigorous and devoted Marxist thinker. Lefebvre claimed that space was as central to the understanding of the workings of human societies as time had been in the eyes of Marx. But space was a special kind of element, both a precondition for the workings of human societies and a social product, which, itself, could shape the nature of human action. When we converse with one another, for example, we do so across space. Conversation, and more generally, social relationships, are human activities that could not occur in the absence of some kind of spatial context. That seems rather obvious. What is less obvious, and what Lefebvre spent a great deal of time exploring, was how different configurations of space were produced by societies. In particular, he argued that under capitalism space was produced in a such a way as to facilitate the workings of capitalism, itself. Ultimately this assertion took a form very germane to our interests as urban sociologists: the space of cities under modern capitalism was configured in such a way as to further and advance the purposes of capitalism, itself.

Such a claim is very profound. Just as Marx would argue that the central tendencies of capitalism are to promote its interests, by virtue of the hegemony of its main ideas, so Lefebvre maintained that the organization of space also, in general, promoted the interests of capitalists at the expense of labor. Consider some simple illustrations of this claim. The human ecologists had argued that key economic and political institutions held land at the center of cities because such groups exercised a dominant role over the life of the city. The center provided the best site from which to exercise such control. Lefebvre would make a similar argument, but would take it a step further, noting that the central location of the city provided the wealthiest capitalists with their best opportunity to dominate the other sectors of society. To Lefebvre, as opposed to the human ecologists, there was nothing natural about the convergence between central location and power: alternative configurations of space were possible with the overthrow and dissolution of capitalism itself. Similarly, the spatial configurations of buildings were done in such a way as to advance the power of the dominant class. Under early industrial capitalism, for example, the workers were arrayed across the floors of factories, and the foremen, the allies of the capitalist owners, were aligned in such a way as to be able to see, and to control, the labor force in the easiest and most effective possible manner.

But Lefebvre's analysis of the nature and workings of space, as a central element of the contemporary world, moved well beyond the dynamics of Marxism. His view, though tied to central elements of Marx's view of the world, opened up a panorama of other possibilities in the analysis of space and different urban forms. He insisted, for example, that one could examine the spatial features of societies in terms of three key elements.[19] The first such element was what he termed the **spatial practices** in societies. This meant the ways in which activities happened in space in particular societies. How did people move about over the course of a day, for example, when they led their lives? Where did they go, how did they move about, what places did they enter and leave, and at what pace did they do so? The second such element was the **representations of space** offered in specific societies. Such representations referred to the way that space was portrayed, or conceived, in particular societies. To Lefebvre, maps were an obvious illustration of this feature of space, both in terms of the elements portrayed by maps and of the different types of maps, e.g. maps of the world, maps of cities, maps for transportation that could be created. Finally, the third element, **representational spaces,** referred to the symbolic, or cultural, constructions made in space by particular societies. They represented the higher and more creative uses of symbols in space, including art and architecture. They also presented the greatest challenge to deciphering, their messages leading to alternative interpretations of their meanings. In sum, there were three major dimensions of space, to Lefebrve, each of which posed its own problems and left its own important traces.

It is important to note here that Lefebvre's dissection of the social nature and production of space does not touch so much on the way that human beings become connected to their positions and settlements in space, that is, places, but rather on the nature of their activities and lives, the pace at which these things occur, and the way they become represented through different forms in space. It is somewhat peculiar that he would ignore this special linkage between humans and points in space, especially because it plays such a large role in the lives of people, whether it is in terms of their memories of residence, or even in their special efforts to celebrate human life at particular sites, such as cemeteries.

Lefebvre did not offer a particular key, or code, for deciphering how the different configurations of space evolved and what they meant, but he provided illustrations of the use of space in different societies and different urban forms, clues to just how significant spatial arrangements were. For example, in describing the configuration of buildings and functions in the Spanish-American town he noted that

> The very building of the towns . . . embodied a plan, which would determine the mode of occupation of the territory and define how it was to be reorganized under the administrative and political authority of urban power. The (*Orders for Discovery and Settlement*))stipulate exactly how the chosen sites ought to be developed. The result is a strictly hierarchical organization of space, a graduate progression outwards from the town's centre, beginning with the *ciudad* and reaching out to the surrounding *pueblos* . . . Each square or rectangular lot has its function assigned to it, while inversely each function is assigned its own place at a greater or lesser distance from the central square; church, administrative buildings, town gates, squares, streets, port installations, warehouses, town hall, and so on. Thus a high degree of segregation is superimposed upon a homogenous space.[20]

Urban space here, then, is produced in such a way as to create a set of conditions within which the life of people is performed – on specific avenues, in buildings, and across the whole course of these constructed elements. To Marx, the set of conditions within which humans carried out their lives was a product of the past in general; to Lefebvre it meant, very precisely, the constructions in space that shaped and dictated the rhythms of everyday life.

Lefebvre's vision of the profound importance of space to our human activities furnishes a new vantage point from which to view the workings of societies, modern capitalism, in particular. And this view, in particular the connection between the dominance of capitalism and the role of space in such dominance, has become the inspiration for a number of other writers who take space as seriously as Lefebvre. They include David Harvey, of course, and also the sociologist Mark Gottdiener. Gottdiener, for instance, has extended the insights of Lefebvre, arguing that under capitalism those specific classes and groups that control key features of space – the land, the buildings – provide a new and dynamic opportunity both for the creation of profit and, of course, for the advancement of capitalism, itself.[21] Gottdiener argues, in particular, that the real estate sector of capitalism, the so-called second circuit of capitalism, provides a rich avenue for profit, and that its dynamics are central to the nature and workings of cities in the contemporary world. He insists that it is in the very nature of capitalism to engage in a restless pursuit and dominance of space, leading to the spatial inequalities within metropolitan areas, between the inner city poverty, and the continuing production of new development in the fringe areas of metropolitan areas. Indeed, Gottdiener argues, it is the production of these new kinds of residential and commercial developments that truly embody Lefebvre's emphasis on the "production of space" under modern capitalism.

Henri Lefebvre has furnished an imaginative and productive way for linking the basic concerns of Marx to our understanding of the operations and development of cities. Moreover, his view opens up a whole set of questions and opportunities in the analysis of space, in general, and cities, in particular. It provides a link and platform from which to view activities ranging from the manner of the transportation of goods in a society, from producer to consumer, to the representation of spatial forms in the architecture of societies.

Manuel Castells

At a very young age, the sociologist, Manuel Castells, made a major mark in scholarship about cities.[22] Castells brought to his task a number of important talents and influences. For one thing, unlike his American counterparts, Castells knew a number of different languages and was thus able to draw together writings about the city not only in English, but also in French and Spanish. For another thing, Castells had been trained in Paris, coming under the influence of major Marxist thinkers of the latter half of the twentieth century, in particular, Louis Althusser and Henri Lefebvre. And for a third, Castells attempted a rather major synthesis, seeking to bridge the abstraction of European social theory with the empiricism of American theory.

The work for which Castells first became famous was a work devoted exclusively to the research and theory about cities.[23] This is actually a very difficult book to grasp, more a set of theoretical reflections and empirical exercises than a systematic theory or empirical analysis. But, like Lefebvre, Castells sets out to understand the nature of the city as urban space, and to try to understand it by incorporating the basic elements of a Marxist framework. Thus, he accepts the building blocks of Marxist theory – the idea of the class struggle, the basic contradictions of capitalism, and the nature of labor and of the need to reproduce labor power in order for capitalism to continue its dominance as the central system of the modern world. The problem he then faces is how to use the Marxist tradition and its concerns to understand the character of the city and urban spaces. The problem is made doubly difficult because, as he acknowledges, Marx had virtually nothing to say about the nature of the city, or about urban spaces.

Castells adopts from Lefebvre the idea that city is really a space, a space that is produced and reproduced through the workings of capitalism. But, unlike Lefebvre, who basically built up his own set of conceptions from scratch, Castells is determined also to review, and then to criticize, virtually all the urban theoretical and empirical research done through the late 1960s. This is a massive undertaking, but it produces some key insights and ideas. Among them is the claim that the Chicago School of Sociology, while producing many important empirical researchers, worked within a theoretical paradigm that limited their understanding both of modern society and of the workings of the city. The ecologists borrowed freely on concepts dealing with population, and features of population growth and decline; but Castells maintains that what really is at work in the development of the city are elements of the struggle and contradictions of modern capitalism – namely the struggle of labor against capital, of workers against managers. Discoveries of the ills and disjunctures of the city, to which ecologists pointed, are really, Castells maintains, the visible problems created by the contradictions of capitalism, itself.

These claims were, in the early 1970s, very novel, and they drew much attention from urban scholars across the world. But the new theoretical framework that Castells proposed to replace the ecological paradigm was neither theoretically coherent nor did it lend itself easily to developing a strong empirical research program. Castells maintained that urban space should be seen as the space within which the reproduction of labor power occurred, that is, the space within which workers lived, consumed and made their way to work on a daily basis. Thus, the nature of transportation must be an important element in studying how laborers live and are treated within the city. But of critical importance, he argued, was the nature of consumption, particularly the nature and means of collective consumption. Consumption could be thought of as what the individual did, but, in the Marxist framework, it really had to do with what the social class did – the collective group of workers, in particular. To examine and develop a strong empirical base for understanding such consumption, Castells, along with colleagues, did empirical research on pubic housing in Paris. He showed the inadequacies of such housing, but also how the state, an accomplice of the capitalist class, provided funds to support such housing. It was thus within the residential conditions of the working class that the Marxist paradigm must direct much of its empirical attention in order to learn more about the nature of urban space under capitalism.

Castells was also aware of the need to study urban politics, in particular, urban social movements that represented the efforts by workers to advance their interests within the urban spaces of capitalism. Such movements were central to the new paradigm because they represented the ways in which the working class might attempt to throw off the yoke of capitalism, and to assert its own rights. In a sense, it represented in the guise of the modern-day society what the workers' revolution had represented to Marx – the effort of the workers to bring the reign of capitalism to an end. But Castells' work in these studies, at least that reported in his first major book, was only at a beginning. In a subsequent work, he devoted far more attention to the nature of social movements, in different cities and at different times, showing how urban dwellers regularly and constantly sought to break out of the constraints of their urban lives.[24]

One of the elements that figured into Castells' thinking about cities, but about capitalism more generally, was that of technology. At various points in his original writings on the city, Castells brings up the central importance of technology:

> the role played by technology in the transformation of urban forms is indisputable. This influence is exercised both through the introduction of new activities of production and consumption and by the almost total elimination of the obstacle **space**, thanks to an enormous development of the means of communication. At the stage of the second industrial revolution, the generalization of electrical energy and the use of the tramway System permitted a widening of the urban concentrations of manpower around ever larger units of industrial production.[25]

This theme of the central importance of technology to understanding the development of modern capitalism ultimately became the focus of Castells' central attention, and the concept of technology displaced that of the city and of urban space, itself. In these writings, Castells advances the thesis that we have entered a new age, the Information Age, and that this period will produce a revolutionary transformation of society.[26] Much like the growth of heavy industry reshaped the world, from cities to countries, the growth of information technology, Castells believes, will also reshape the world. Indeed, it already has begun to do so, he argues. It provides links among people and places across the globe, providing the almost instantaneous transfer of varying forms of information, from news to financial data. The rapid flows of information, in a "timeless time," Castells argues, has a number of central consequences, among them, a weakening of state sovereignty and a growing strength of various kinds of networks – of people, organizations, and especially financial institutions.

This is a time, Castells maintains, when a variety of novel things are taking place in the world. They include various kinds of social movements, from the anti-globalization movement to the Zapatistas in Mexico. These are no longer simply the movements of the working classes against the bourgeoisie, nor of Socialists against capitalists. They defy any easy description, or any simple enumeration of their strategies. What they hold in common, however, is that they seem to be local reactions to the emergence and development of global forces, especially of global capitalism. Moreover, like capitalists themselves, they rely on the same rapid and easy flow of communications, whether across the Internet or via fax machines. More than that, the new social movements are also concerned about new issues, especially about issues of what Castells refers to as "identity." Older social movements were engaged in seeking to overthrow the capitalists, whereas many newer social movements are primarily concerned with forging an identity among the participants themselves, whether that be an identity based on their common ethnicity, or an identity based upon a common concern with the evils of globalization, itself.

Castells' arguments about this age, like his first ones about cities, take him across a wide range of materials and many countries. He is convinced, however, that this new age will replace the age of industry, and that it will leave many changes in its wake. Among them are changes that will have substantial implications for the use of space. While rapid communications means that the distances across space no longer hold the meaning they once did, the technology of such communications, and its concentration in certain specific locales, will change the nature of cities, and living spaces, in general. For example, Castells, like many others, argues that the use of the computer, and the hook-up to the Internet, will mean that people no longer have to spend most of their day at a central work location. In fact, many can, and are, working directly from their homes, thereby displacing the need or importance of work space outside the home. In addition, the concentration of technology, and of its supports in finance and banking, mean that new urban centers will grow up, organized around the new technology. Here, Castells has in mind sites like Silicon Valley, and Austin, Texas, home to the Dell Computer Corporation. Finally, he argues that there will be a continuing growth of large urban centers, new "mega-cities," in which more and more people will be concentrated. Shanghai, Mexico City, Paris, Hong Kong, and a host of other cities now represent such centers. And, because of their size, and, especially, their economic importance, they will develop a degree of autonomy from the states in which they lie, in effect, becoming sovereign urban empires, something like the city-states of Venice and Florence of the Middle Ages.

Castells' latest writings are clearly his most original and forceful. They have inspired a great deal of commentary, and are likely to shape our understanding of how the future will unfold. Most of all, they suggest an urban future likely to be very different from that of the urban past – where, in fact, the nature and use of urban space simply will be vastly different. It remains to be seen, however, how the city, itself, will look. The old industrial city surely will disappear – the one in which businesses were housed at the center, and workers, lacking transportation, were compelled to live nearby. Already, we can observe new cities forming at the outskirts of old cities, particularly in more advanced economies like that of the United States. But will the city only expand, losing its central forces? Or, will it simply become a sprawl, one commercial and residential development after another scattered across space? Stay tuned.

David Harvey

If Manuel Castells proved to be the stimulus for a major rethinking about the manner in which cities ought to be studied, with his emphasis on a study of the nature of consumption and the various forms of class struggle in urban areas, the geographer, David Harvey, proved to be the more systematic and ultimately more influential Marxist writing about the city. Trained in the conventional form of geographic science, Harvey underwent a certain kind of theoretical metamorphosis, which he outlined and described at some length in his first major Marxist work, *Social Justice and the City*.[27] Harvey argued essentially that if a scholar were interested in studying and understanding the wide range of features of urban life in the modern world, there was no better thinker to whom to turn than Marx. "I do not turn to [Marx's analysis]," he wrote, "out of some . . . sense of its inherent superiority . . . but because I can find no other way of accomplishing what I set out to do or of understanding what has to be understood."[28] A Marxist view of city life, which meant beginning from fundamental principles, namely, that under capitalism capitalists appropriated the surplus produced by workers, could lead, Harvey argued, into all sorts of interesting insights into the nature of urban life.

Yet, like Castells, Harvey would struggle mightily with how to make Marx relevant to understanding the nature of urban life. Marx wrote about factories, and the struggle between the owners and the workers. He wrote about the underlying theory of value and surplus value, and the manner in which the labor of the laborers were lost in the production process as the owners of industry paid them, in effect, for much less than they produced. He provided a compelling theory of how profits came about under modern capitalism, and how the engine of capitalism constantly was driven forward by the effort to secure ever-greater profit. But what possible bearing, or connection, could such arguments as these have on understanding the nature of urban life?

Over the years, Harvey has managed to wrest from Marx certain key ideas, and to extend other ones, in a way that makes Marx meaningful to modern metropolitan life.[29] He has argued, for example, that the basic distinction Marx drew in his analysis of **commodities** provides a very productive way for gaining insight into the struggles between residents and capitalists in the modern city.[30] Marx argued that the products of capitalism take on two values – a value as a commodity, and thus a thing to be exchanged in the market; and a value as use, and thus a thing to be used by its owners. Now a powerful tension emerges here within each and every commodity that is thus produced under modern capitalism. People who possess the commodity wish to put it to certain uses. The laborer owns his labor-power and wishes to uses it for his own good, but the capitalist, in employing the laborer, also purchases his laborer-power and thus can put it to whatever use he, the capitalist, wishes. Herein, in part, lies the source of the class struggle under capitalism. The laborer wishes to use his labor-power and its products for his own good, but the capitalist, having purchased his labor-power, now owns it. And because laborers are only minimally supported for their effort under capitalism, they must constantly re-employ themselves, and thus forever be at the mercy of the capitalist owners and industrialists.

If, then, one thinks of the nature of the city in terms of commodities, such as land and houses, one can easily import the nature of the class struggle into urban life, and uncover a host of previously undiscovered tendencies. Struggles between homeowners and developers, Harvey informs us, have to do with the effort of homeowners to want to use their land and homes versus the developers who wish to simply purchase such lands to be used as another form of commodity.[31] Tensions between residents and business firms over certain areas, and zones within the city, again can be seen in the light of a fundamental tension, defined by the nature of commodities, between the residents who wish to use the features of the city for themselves, and the business firms that wish to make a profit through the sale of these same areas.

Harvey's use of Marx's conception of commodities proved productive not only to his own work but to that of other scholars as well.[32] Harvey also extended Marx's theories by moving beyond Marx's preoccupation with production under capitalism – a preoccupation connected directly to the developments he, himself, observed – to consider other ways and forms of making profit, particularly those connected to urban life. Thus, Harvey has written about the three different **circuits of capitalism**, drawing here, in part, on the work of Lefebvre.[33] He argues that there are different forms of production and profit making under capitalism, not that, alone, connected to the creation of surplus value by workers in industry. There is the first circuit of capitalism, which is concerned with the basic processes of production and consumption, and which formed the heart of Marx's analysis of capitalism. But there is also a second circuit of capitalism, that circuit which is directly connected with the built environment of cities – buildings, roads, modes of transportation and the like.[34] And there is also a third circuit of capitalism, the scientific knowledge that is produced and used to make capitalism work better.

Now, Harvey suggests, while Marx argued that the engine of capitalism was driven by the surplus created in the first circuit, in fact, the second circuit also provides an avenue for surplus and profit. In particular, those who

invest in land and other forms of real estate, like buildings, ca┊
investments also to make profit for themselves. It is no┊
businessperson who runs a manufacturing company, but also ┊
who invests in real estate, and the developer, who creates new res ┄┄┄┄ ┄┄
commercial developments, who also can turn an important profit. Moreover, under certain conditions of crisis, in particular, when factories have over-
produced goods in capitalism, thus driving profits down, the system itself
can seek and find new opportunities for investment in land. Land and real
estate, then, provide almost a safety valve for the cyclical nature of modern
capitalism, another avenue for profit. And it is a key avenue, from the urban
student's point of view, for the construction and reconstruction of real estate
and buildings is what urban life is all about. Thus, Harvey suggests, one gains
a key insight not only into modern capitalism, but also into the **built environment** of cities, by realizing that they are built and developed, in large
part, through the continuing effort of capitalism to find ways to extend and
expand itself.

Harvey, in brief, has managed to rework Marx to make his ideas far more
relevant to the study of the city and to modern life than Marx himself managed. The city, thus, becomes a window for understanding not only urban
life, but for also understanding the new forms and avenues for class struggles. The decay of the inner core of modern cities, coupled with the growth of
suburban areas, is part and parcel of a kind of uneven development fostered
by modern capitalism.[35] It is not the case that the families and workers within
the inner cities do not want work, but rather that business goes where it can
make a profit, and where it can find workers who will help it make such a
profit. Moreover, housing developments take place in the outer fringes of
urban areas precisely because this is where the value of housing will be the
highest – and where developers and their bankers also can make the greatest profits for their investments. In brief, the city, looked at through the eyes
of modern Marxist writers, like David Harvey, becomes something of a profit-
engine, driven to find and exploit sources of revenue wherever it can. And it
does so, Harvey contends, in a systematic and ruthless manner, leaving no
home unturned.

STRENGTHS AND WEAKNESSES

The neo-Marxist paradigm for the analysis of space and urban forms represents the most theoretically provocative and coherent paradigm today. Based
on the rich and theoretically profound insights of Marx, it has unlimited potential for the analysis of cities, and the different forms they take. In the hands
of such imaginative interpreters as Castells, Harvey and, especially, Lefebvre,
it also furnishes endless opportunities for gaining insight into the workings

of modern capitalism, particularly into the different and powerful arrangements of space and its social production by such agents as real estate brokers and developers.

Its weaknesses begin with the general weaknesses of the Marxist paradigm, itself. Is production the key moment, repeated over and over, in the unfolding and development of social life? If one believes that it is, then the writings of Marx, as extended by figures like Harvey, provide a powerful method of analysis of cities, and of the varying battles waged within them, between real estate developers and homeowners, employers and workers, the inner city poor and the suburban rich. Yet the basic failure of Marx, and of his followers, is at times to put too much emphasis on the economy, and production, and too little on the possibility that other institutional forms, such as the local government or cultural institutions, can exercise a power over the life of cities and their residents. Modern society has become extraordinarily diverse since the time of Marx, with a much greater variety of different groups, besides social classes, and different forces exercising their power over cities and larger metropolitan regions. Both Harvey and Castells recognized these changes, but it was only Lefebvre who began to move Marx into profoundly new directions in the analysis of space. If the neo-Marxist paradigm is to survive, indeed, to thrive, it seems to us that it must move in the directions laid out for it by Henri Lefebvre.

The City as a Growth Machine

Today one of the most popular interpretations of the nature of urban life, and the city in America, in particular, is known as the theory of the "city as a **growth machine**." This view was developed in the mid-1970s by sociologist Harvey Molotch, and drew its inspiration, in part, from a somewhat modified Marxist view of the city. But Molotch took a slightly different route to his analysis than the one taken by the neo-Marxist analysts.

Until the mid-1970s, the analysis of urban politics had been guided by an American paradigm, more or less developed by the political scientist, Robert Dahl.[36] Dahl argued that American politics could best be understood as the product of various and diverse forces, each of which was roughly equal in power to that of the other. This argument, known as the **pluralist** interpretation of American politics, insisted, in particular, that the politics of urban areas involved a number of competing forces, no one of which was especially dominant. On issues of schools, he argued, for example, that the various groups concerned with educational issues, ranging from local Parent–Teachers Associations to school administrators, ultimately shaped such decisions. On issues of urban development, however, another array of participants became involved, often the federal government but also local officials such as the mayor. The urban polity, in other words, was one in which different issues arose, and in the case of each there was an array of different participants that made its influence felt.

The 1970s, however, were a time when all such arguments came under the microscope for critical analysis, and the pluralist view was no exception. Molotch, just out of graduate school at the University of Chicago (and hence well-versed in the human ecological paradigm) took exception both to Dahl's view and to that of the human ecologists. He argued, in particular, that the politics of cities in America were all about urban growth – no more, no less. While issues such as education or urban development were important, the critical issue to all cities was whether they grew, or not. In other words, the basic goal of cities was quite simple: grow, or be left in the dust of developers who move their operations to other cities.[37]

Molotch expanded on his insight to argue that the goal of "urban growth" was one that was fostered by a number of different key groups in the city. The real estate sector was pivotal inasmuch as such specific groups as realtors, developers and bankers all were involved in promoting the sale and development of land, and thus the basic expansion of the city. Those who owned and rented land, in particular, the class of **rentiers**, Molotch argued, were central to the expansion of the city for they sought endlessly to expand their holdings and to drive up the rental price on those holdings. But a variety of leading urban forces also came into play, including local government and its officials as well as the local media. Molotch argued persuasively that these various forces together became a "growth coalition," a coalition whose self-interest lay in the continuing and endless expansion of the American city. On the face of it, his argument was a very plausible one, indeed.[38] American cities, particularly those in the newer sections of the country, like the Southwest and West, seemed to be involved in an endless game of competing with one another to grow the fastest and the largest. Moreover, everywhere one looked, urban growth was a goal around which there emerged a strong and powerful consensus, built from the collective efforts of developers, bankers, mayors and the local media.

A decade after his first article, Molotch teamed with sociologist John Logan to produce an award-winning book that extended the argument further.[39] In this work, they drew more directly from the neo-Marxist paradigm, particularly the writings of David Harvey. Following Harvey (and Marx), they argued that the basic elements of land and space in the city could be thought of as commodities, thus having both a **use-value** and an **exchange-value**. Herein, too, they parlayed a basic contradiction of the modern capitalist city in America, namely, that property-owners, or residents, wanted to use their land and neighborhoods in one fashion, but that such a use-value came into conflict with the interests of real estate brokers and developers who wanted simply to exploit land for its profit. Moreover, Logan and Molotch extended the notion of use-value further, suggesting that there were several uses to which the land of residents and the neighborhood, in general, could be put, including not only as a place for a home but also a place for recreation and daily activities. By putting the Marxian notion of commodities to such a use in the modern American city, Logan and Molotch were then able to identify a powerful and revealing underlying tension, one that helped explain to many observers some of the basic tensions of the modern city.

Not surprisingly, the notion of the city as a growth machine has become a very popular device for explaining both the modern American city and the nature of its politics. Indeed, a count of the various citation indices reveals it to be the most popular and influential paradigm, at least among sociologists, today. But it has flaws, the major one of which is that it fails to pay close attention to the changing history of American cities, as well as to differences among cities located in different sections of the country. Orum, in particular, has shown that different agents and institutions have played varying roles in the growth of American cities throughout history. Sometimes it is real estate entrepreneurs who lead such growth, but sometimes it also has been the local government, as the driving institution. Moreover, the notion of growth, at all costs, is one that has been most visible in the newly developing regions of America, and much less evident in the older industrial regions. Finally, the argument, while elegant and persuasive, has proven to be only useful in explaining the growth of American cities. For whatever reasons, it has both cultural and national limitations, deriving perhaps mainly from the fact that America is a nation in which the market has driven real estate development, and urban growth, more directly than in other nations.

Cities as Symbolic Economies: The Invention and Re-invention of Place

Whether we choose to look at cities through the eyes of a human ecologist, or a neo-Marxist, or even a growth machine advocate, our focus will always be on the workings of the dominant economic and political institutions. Human ecologists inquire into such elements as the movement and growth of the local population, but they are keen enough to realize that these changes happen in part because of the workings of the local economy.[40] Neo-Marxists emphasize the relentless expansion of capitalism across metropolitan areas, producing a kind of uneven development, in which some areas, like the inner city, become impoverished, whereas others, like the suburban fringes, bask in the sunshne of new jobs and new mansions. And those who look at the city as a growth machine marvel continuously at the ever-expanding region of the city, noting how such expansion not only fulfills the interests of dominant business and political groups but how it often comes at the expense of neighborhoods and their residents.

Yet however sharp and wide-angled the lenses of such paradigms are, they also neglect many important features of the urban area. They fail, for example, to explore the rich diversity of architectural forms in cities, concentrating their efforts, instead, mainly on the number and value of new commercial and residential developments. They often take little note of the meaning of the rich array of new public places to be found in urban areas, ranging from parks to hotels to the vibrant skyscrapers in major metropolitan areas. In effect, they sacrifice diversity for uniformity, quality for quantity, culture for economics.

Nevertheless in the past two decades or so, scholars have begun to take the symbolic forms of cities very seriously. In large part what they have attempted is to connect such things as the architecture and symbolic paraphernalia of the city to the broader economic and political forces of the contemporary world. These forms of symbolism – the cultures of cities – have come to be seen not simply as incidental to the nature of urban life but as often representing its very essence. Thus, unlike the ecologists, who argue that we should look merely at the population growth and kind of people who live in cities, students of urban culture insist that we also study the kinds of buildings and advertisements that line city streets, the forms of new museums, the ways that people consume, the themes that are used to create to new suburban developments, and other such representations both of the city and of the kinds of people who live there.

Foremost among such students of urban culture is the sociologist Sharon Zukin. Zukin has spent the past twenty years observing and reflecting on the different symbolic attributes of urban life.[41] She seeks to combine an emphasis on the material side of urban life, particularly the ways in which capitalism shapes the city, with an emphasis on the cultural, or symbolic, side. Moreover, her work is devoted to exploring the ways in which the city has changed, particularly over the course of the twentieth century. Like David Harvey and Manuel Castells, she sees the city as having been created by the forces of capitalism. But she is also very attentive to the ways in which capitalism has changed and developed, especially to the ways in which the loss of industry and the rise of financial capital have reshaped the city, particularly in the latter half of the twentieth century.

Much of Zukin's writing has been about New York City, a place where she has lived and worked for many years. In her earliest book, she explored the changes that had taken place in Manhattan over the course of many decades, from the early twentieth century to the 1970s. Like many other American cities, New York had lost a number of industries, some of which simply closed down, others of which moved abroad or to other regions of the United States. But, she noted, the loss of manufacturing industries was not simply a structural change, but something that served the interests of dominant social and political elites in New York City as well. Such groups actually conspired to change the city from a center of manufacturing to a center both of upscale residences and of finance.

A leading, though unwitting, sector in this transformation were the many artists who lived and worked in New York City. By the 1960s, former manufacturing lofts became residences and work spaces for many artists; old manufacturing areas, such as SoHo, now became strong cultural presences in the city, the places where cutting-edge artwork was produced and sold. Art now became a strong force of production in the city, replacing the old industrial form. Yet the movement created by the artists soon overtook them, and real estate developers began to market loft living to the middle- and upper-classes. A whole new group of urban dwellers arose in places like SoHo, and many other downtown American cities as well, a group of people who became known as the "gentrifiers," wealthy people many of whom chose to move back to the city from the suburbs. The artists, who had replaced the industrialists in the lofts, now found themselves displaced, many times forced to live in poorer dwellings simply because they had been priced out of the loft market.

Over time, Zukin has paid more and more attention to these cultural shifts and transformations in the city, trying to show the ways in which they are linked to the changing nature of capitalism. For example, in recent years the downtown areas of many cities have been altered by the growing number of new immigrants who have settled in or nearby them. The immigrants do not merely bring in new numbers of residents, as the demographers would suggest, but they alter the very cultural fabric of the city as well. As Zukin shows, they have created a new symbolic economy, the centerpiece of which is the many new restaurants and shopping markets created by the new immigrants. Such imports as these have begun to refashion the tastes of Americans by providing entirely new and different forms of cuisine but also an array of different items and goods from abroad. The downtowns, not only of New York City, but also of smaller sites like Brooklyn, have been refashioned over time, from primarily manufacturing centers to primarily centers of consumption and of shopping. In a sense these urban transformations presage but also signify the major structural changes to the American economy, from an industrial economy to a service economy. And with such a major change, Zukin argues, the variety and diversity of cultural forms take on a new meaning, and new significance, in shaping and framing the postindustrial city.

Once art and culture rise to such prominence, they can become an au-

Plate 2.1 The theming of America: The Las Vegas Eiffel Tower at night. Photo courtesy of Ethan Miller/Las Vegas Sun.

tonomous force in making and remaking the space around us. To Zukin, like a number of other urban observers, the prototype of the modern cultural landscape is to be found in places such as the imaginary fantasylands of Disney World and Disneyland.[42] What happens in such sites is that an effort has been made to create a set of visually stimulating symbols and pleasurable experiences intended to make visitors feel happy and content. The fairytale stories that we have learned about Mickey Mouse and his fellow cinematic creatures come to life on the stage and in other public displays in the world of Disney. There are wonderful rides and marvelous adventures, delicious food; indeed, there is such an array of things to delight our senses that we can stay there for days, taking a respite from the hard work of our everyday lives. The Disney sites represent the very essence of cultural workings in the modern world. They are fabricated places that invite us to engage in fantasy, intended to be more captivating than the real places where we live and work. They are designed to appeal to our desire to consume rather than to produce experiences, to be voyeurs rather than participants in life. And, not so incidentally, they provide a uniform content so that a person can connect to a Disney World not only in America but also in Europe or Hong Kong. In this regard they become like the other common capitalist coin of our era, whether it be a McDonald's in Shanghai or a Starbucks in Moscow.

Features of the Disney experience can be found more generally in the urban experience in the modern world, so Zukin maintains. Many cities have turned essentially from places of production (the steel towns of yesterday) to ones of consumption (the Las Vegas of today). The work of architects and restaurateurs, retail shops and public parks, takes the form of providing a rich display of materials to entertain and to amuse us. Contemporary architects, like Frank Gehry, who is perhaps the premiere architect of the current period, constructs buildings that are eclectic ensembles of different styles and forms. Large metal boxes are juxtaposed to swirls of glass, the total result of which represents the kind of eclecticism that many analysts of culture see in our "**postmodern** world." Zukin examines these kinds of urban phenomena, drawing out of them not merely their rich meanings but how, in their odd juxtaposition, they portray some of the fragmentation and chaos evident in the rapid change now taking place in many cities. Indeed, such time-intensifying and space-bending change, characteristic of our new age of technology, is a major cultural theme that Zukin explores. She finds it evident not only in temporary stability of an old steel town but also in the constant rise and fall of the built environment – its **creative destruction** – across the modern metropolitan landscape. And she traces the roots of all of this in the engine of capitalism, an engine whose workings, she believes, are not to be found simply in dollars and cents but also in the oddly shaped towers and obelisks of urban form.

The cultural forms of modern urban life are equally important to the work of Mike Davis, one of the most visible and controversial students of cities. Most of Davis' work has been concerned with exploring the rich interior of modern-day Los Angeles. Davis writes about Los Angeles from a variety of angles, emphasizing the literature of the city but also its dominant architectural forms.[43] He, himself, sees Los Angeles from its darker sides, from what he terms the "noir" style of writing not only about the city but also in the form of Hollywood films. The "noir" style emphasizes the brutal and anonymous forces of urban life rather than the friendlier features; it is a city of the night rather than of the day. Thus, for example, Davis writes about the form that new museums or gated communities take in Los Angeles, noting how they appear to be walled fortresses, designed to keep out the unholy masses and to protect their residents with a kind of constant surveillance. Drawing on the work of Michel Foucault, the leading postmodern thinker of the contemporary era, Davis notes how television cameras are designed to survey the landscape of local areas, providing police with a way of keeping the residents under control. Like Zukin, he also looks to modern architects, such as Frank Gehry, to provide some insight into how modern urban forms come about and what they represent.

Cultural analysts, such as Zukin and Davis, take seriously the admonition of Henri Lefebvre to examine carefully the production of urban space in the modern city – not only how it is produced but the way its forms create and shape the workings of contemporary life.[44] They also furnish us with the beginnings of a kind of language within which we can talk and think about urban form. Although capitalism continues to be the driving force behind the endless growth and destruction of different sections of the modern city, the forms in which it does its work also matters. Tall glass-lined perpendicular skyscrapers fashion one kind of city, and one kind of life both for residents and for workers: power lies at the top in such places, and a simple kind of uniformity describes the rules by which its occupants will live. By contrast, suburban areas in which there is a rich array of different architectural styles, ranging from a ranch house to an old Victorian home, speak volumes about a different kind of life – of wealth, diversity, uniqueness, a strong willingness to preserve historical artifacts and, of course, the presence both of municipal and individual autonomy. It is the attention to these varied and rich kinds of cultural forms – the specific sites where we live and where we work – that are the bread and butter of the cultural analysts of modern urban life, and to which we must also attend if we are to fully understand the nature of the city.

STRENGTHS AND WEAKNESSES

The analysis of the cultural forms of urban life represents a rich field of data and insights waiting to be mined by urban social scientists. Public art and urban architecture, new forms of urban communities, the rich visual display of graffiti and wall murals, the new shopping malls to be found everywhere, these and many forms tell us as much about the life of cities today as the balance sheet of modern capitalism. The strength of such analysis lies in the attention to visual and other aesthetic features of the urban milieu, elements that help to create for us a full sense of the city and of specific places within it. The main drawback to this perspective is that it possesses no easy language or framework that we can transport and use freely to get a reading on the nature of the city (see Lefebvre on this issue). What are we to look for when we read the symbols of the city? What form, or type, of culture is most important in the creation of modern urban life. And do these forms not only shape our sense of the modern city but also create a unique kind of place? These are the kinds of questions that remain to be addressed by the cultural analysis of urban life, but they are questions so powerful as to prompt, one would hope, more and more social scientists to answer them.

Historical/Institutional Views of the City

The penultimate perspective that we shall consider is one that draws it main inspirations from the writings of Max Weber. Though Weber, as an analyst of the city, was primarily concerned with the rise and development of the medieval city-states, such as Venice and Florence, it is his general approach as a social scientist that has served as important guide for some recent work on the nature of cities.

Weber's main emphasis as a scholar was to disavow general abstract theory, such as that of Marx, in favor of more carefully refined and considered historical analyses. Though he believed, along with Marx, that the forces of capitalism dominated the modern age, he also believed that the social scientist must make every effort to pin down his analyses and conclusions in clear historical facts. The contingencies of history, the specific workings of institutions and of various groups of men and women, were more central to an understanding of the world, according to Weber, than some abstract theorizing. Abstract theories were fine, in their place, but, as he once pointed out, they represented a beginning not the conclusion of any analysis of historical details.

Some recent students of cities have taken this general approach to the social sciences to heart. Historian Kenneth Jackson, for example, in a landmark study of suburbs in America, has traced the historical growth of post-World War II suburban development to a number of fairly specific though fundamental features of American society.[45] For example, he points out that suburban development after the war relied heavily on the availability of loans to veterans from the Federal Housing Authority. Those loans permitted veterans to buy homes cheaply, but they also permitted developers to produce a range of new housing on the outskirts of metropolitan areas. Here was a key case in which the federal government (or the state) played a major role in the patterns of urbanization in America, but it was a role that could be tied to a specific set of policies and a specific time, not to some kind of general *deus ex machina* in the workings of government. Likewise the historian Erik Monkonnen believes that the urban development in America can be traced to the growth of major urban institutions, such as the police force, the fire department and local government. Hence, he devotes a good deal of attention to tracing how these public agencies developed in the late nineteenth century, noting their activities came to shape the ebb and flow of urban life in America.[46]

Such work as this, on the city, is absolutely critical to gaining a fuller understanding of the nature of cities and of the process of urbanization, in general. A broadly based form of this kind of work was done by one of us.[47] Orum, in particular, was interested in understanding the general ways in which the **institutions** of cities developed in America, and how cities might have changed over time, particularly in terms of the forces that drove the growth of cities. He undertook an in-depth study of one American city, in particular, Milwaukee, Wisconsin, in an effort to understand the specific forces that were involved in this city's emergence. By focusing carefully on the origins of the city, and by tracing its growth from its beginnings in the early nineteenth century to the late twentieth century he was able to show important transformations in the nature of the city over time.

Specifically, he maintained that over the course of its 150-year life, different agents and institutions at different points in time dominated the growth of Milwaukee. Early on, real estate entrepreneurs were the key agents for growth, those who bought and sold land for profit. Not only did they promote and expand the fortunes of the city, but, because of their very visibility they also became the first leading public officials elected to the office of mayor. Soon thereafter, the forces of the industrial revolution reshaped the city. Now new industries became the main spur to growth, prompting not only tens of thousands of new jobs but also leading to the development of a strong set of private industrial institutions in the city. Such institutions, and their leaders, served as the leading edge for growth, far overshadowing the rather primitive and fragile forces of local government. But over time the engine of the local economy cooled off and, as it did so, the forces of local government became more prominent. By the early part of the twentieth century, in fact, local government had become the key player, promoting the growth of Milwaukee. Its officials played a hand in seeking to extend the city's territory, sometimes successfully annexing new areas but often being rebuffed by its adjacent suburbs. So deep did the division become between the city of Milwaukee and its neighbors that it set into motion a long-term antagonism, one that continues to this very day.

By the latter half of the twentieth century, major decline set into Milwaukee, prompted in large part by the growing decline of local industries. Deep social divisions were evident in the city, divisions between the owners and management of local industry and local workers and their unions. Strikes and conflicts ensued over the course of the 1940s and 1950s, and then, much as in other American industrial cities, the industries simply packed up their plants and moved elsewhere. It was not simply a matter of local capitalism exploiting local workers: it was also a matter that unions, having forced up local wages, contributed to their own demise as plants and firms decided they could make more profits elsewhere – abroad or in the South – where no such union wages were demanded.

The history of Milwaukee, which parallels many other industrial cities, reveals the specific and concrete ways in which the larger forces of capitalism, and local government, came into being, and also came into conflict. Orum argues that rather than elevating the forces of capitalism, or government, to some kind of pre-eminent role in a general theory, attention must be rather paid to the way that such institutions emerge, and how their actions unfold in a specific set of circumstances over time. Historical contingency is important, in his eyes, precisely because history is not simply a set of determined structures but also leaves openings, openings for different groups to take action that can turn the tide against social structures. For example, while Orum notes that the process of loss of industry, or deindustrialization, in Milwaukee happened in many other similar cities, he also argues that how city officials and industrialists responded could have made life much easier for local residents, particularly workers.

The general lesson of the historical/institutional view of the city is that one must attend to the workings of broad social forces, whether of modern capitalism or the government, but always do so with an eye to how those forces actually work in specific circumstances. Cities, Orum insists, each have their unique histories and circumstances, and often such unique qualities are as important to the lives of residents as are the more general patterns. In other words, one might say, place matters – particularly to the lives of local residents.

STRENGTHS AND WEAKNESSES

The strength of this approach is that it provides a very concrete way of studying cities, and particularly of understanding them in terms of their historical development. It takes the more general lessons, offered by abstract theories, and uses them to disclose the concrete operations of specific places. It eschews broad abstract theory in favor of more grounded and concrete understanding of local circumstances, but with an eye to the importance of history.

The weaknesses of this approach are that it can often lead the scholar/ scientist to become so enraptured with historical detail as to lose sight of the broader lessons at work. This is often the danger of much historical research on cities, particularly if it is not guided by some more general inquiry or question. Another danger is that each city, in particular, its history and institutions, is taken to be so unique that it becomes next to impossible to understand what general lessons it has to offer to the urban analyst. In brief, then, historical/institutional analyses must guard against the opposite danger of abstract theories – the danger of detail, of becoming convinced that history is all contingencies and no general process.

Global Perspectives: The City is no Longer Local

The perspectives we have presented and critiqued thus far tend to focus on the city as a discrete local system or unit in the national context, especially in Western industrialized countries. Accelerated **globalization** through increasing interactions between economies and cultures over the past two decades, however, has greatly influenced various aspects of the city, or completely reshaped them in some cases. Put differently, the impact of globalization has turned the city's traditional intra-national and local orientations outward to the international economy. Once the city has been to large extent denationalized, it is no longer local in its existence and functions.

Nevertheless, the impact of globalization on the city is uneven across national contexts. While a few have emerged as global cities as dominant financial centers, others have become partially integrated with the global economy, with still others, especially some cities in developing countries being only marginally connected to the outside world. This uneven local impact is also reflected in the differentiation of cities within and across national urban systems. In this section, we introduce and evaluate the scholarship that takes different global perspectives on and associated analytic approaches to the city.

The scholar who laid the historical groundwork for global perspectives on the city is the eminent British geographer, Peter Hall, who first published the book *The World Cities* in 1966.[48] Simply suggesting that world cities are national centers of government, trade, and professional talents of all kinds, Hall focused on eight such cities: New York, London, Tokyo, Paris, Randstad Holland (the sprawling urban complex that includes Amsterdam, Rotterdam, and The Hague), Moscow, Hong Kong, and Mexico City. It was unfortunate that Hall's idea did not become more widely accepted until the early and mid-1980s when geographer John Friedmann advanced a more refined research agenda for world cities. Friedmann suggested that world cities are a small number of massive urban regions at the apex of the global urban hierarchy that exercise worldwide control over production and market expansion. With their global control functions directly reflected in the structure of their production sectors and employment, world cities also are major sites for the concentration and accumulation of international capital. Friedmann identified as world cities New York, London, Tokyo, Paris, Randstad Holland, Hong Kong, Mexico City (Peter Hall's world cities), and a number of other major international cites.[49] Friedmann's work marked the beginning and continuation of research on world or global cities through the 1980s and into the 1990s.

Sociologist Saskia Sassen, with the publication of the book *The Global City: New York, London, Tokyo* in 1991, brought a definitive touch to the study of the **global city** through a sharp conceptualization and a systematic comparison of three such cities.[50] According to Sassen, global cities function as (1) highly concentrated command points in the organization of the world economy; (2) key locations for finance and specialized services, which have replaced manufacturing as the leading industries; (3) innovative sites of production in these leading industries; and (4) markets for the products and innovations of these industries.[51] From Sassen's perspective, the hallmark of a global city is the growth and extent of its producer services, which include accounting, banking, financial services, legal services, insurance, real estate, computer and information processing, etc. Producer services are highly concentrated in the central locations in cities of considerable size because they require a diversified resource base, centrality of information, and easy access to the concentration of headquarters of large manufacturing firms.[52] Having identified these clear criteria and characteristics of the global city, Sassen also has examined such major international cities as Miami, Toronto, and Sydney, which exercise global city functions but are nevertheless not global cities themselves.[53] Of a number of insights and contributions from Sassen's work, a central proposition stands out: the dominant influence of global cities coexists with undesirable local consequences such as the growing income equality between white-collar professionals in high-paying producer services jobs and minority workers in low-end commercial services and the striking spatial disparity between the booming downtown through renewal and the physical decay of peripheral areas.[54]

By taking this kind of global perspective on the city, Sassen and others have questioned the fundamental assumption of the city as a bounded territory of the sovereign state and pointed to the critical need to reconceptualize the relationship between local place and global space.[55] Instead of seeing the city as a bounded unit, Sassen argues that it is now a node in a grid of cross-boundary processes.[56] While acknowledging the powerful impact of globalization, some geographers and sociologists have emphasized the persistence of local diversity. British geographers Ash Amin and Nigel Thrift suggested that global imperatives inevitably encounter places with distinctive, historically layered, socioeconomic structures and traditions. Therefore, globalization does not imply sameness between places, but a continuation of the significance of territorial diversity and difference. Sociologist McMichael labels this local diversity in the global order as "local cosmopolitanism."[57] Regardless of these somewhat divergent arguments, there seems to be little doubt that the city now must be studied from global perspectives and in a global context.

The recent urban literature has clearly reflected this conceptual shift. Stimulated by the globalization scholarship in general and Saskia Sassen's global city perspective in particular, urban scholars have conducted in-depth case studies on a diverse number of US and international cities concerning the local impact of globalization and the cities' responses to it. The topics and foci include local politics in a global era, globalization and residential segregation, globalization, immigration, and suburban differentiation, globalization and inequalities, and so forth. The cases range from the heavily studied cites of New York, Los Angeles, Chicago, and Tokyo to the relatively understudied cities of Brussels, Calcutta, and Rio de Janeiro.[58] These case studies of individual cities have revealed considerable variation in how global economic and cultural forces could reshape local traditions and development. More importantly, these case studies provide lessons on the capacity of cities or lack of it to resist or counter globalization based on diverse local strengths and weaknesses.

If the city is no longer local but is embedded in a global system, this relational structure must be theoretically accounted for and empirically demonstrated. Despite its explicit theoretical effort, Sassen's global city perspective, which focuses on the top cities in the global economic hierarchy, does not offer a complete account of the latter's relational attributes. By examining individual cities in the global context, the comparative case approach mentioned above missed out on the systematic features of the global urban hierarchy. This scholarly challenge has been partly met by an alternative global perspective on and approach to the city. Drawing insights from world-systems theory of Immanuel Wallerstein,[59] sociologists David Smith and Michael Timberlake proposed a political economy/global network perspective that a vast network of locales tied together by multiple direct exchanges constitutes a world city system.[60] They also suggested that the relations among cities are complex but observable and reflect the relative positions and power of core vs. peripheral cities, and studying these inter-city relations is important for understanding the world system itself, especially its inherent inequality.[61]

This global relational or systemic perspective on the city reinforces but moves beyond the case-based global theorizing and research on the city. It is consistent with Sassen's global city perspective by emphasizing the dena-tionalization of the city. Instead of the nation-state, which has been weak-ened by globalization, the city, or more importantly, the relations among cities across national boundaries, have become the unit and focus of study. Going beyond the global city perspective, which focuses almost exclusively on few global cities as the core of the global urban hierarchy, the global rela-tional perspective deals with both core and peripheral cities by locating them in the relative positions of the global economy and demonstrating the extent of ties between them. The crucial analytic concept here is the dominance or power of a city in a system based on how it is positioned in relation to other cities through direct and indirect ties. In other words, a city of centrality is generally a key node in a network of extensive ties. Methodologically, this is a network approach that uses quantitative data to model the frequency and strength of any kind of connections among cities and thus arriving at conclusions about the structural characteristics of a given city hierarchy or system.

Thus far, much of the rigorous analysis and empirical findings through this approach have been associated with the work by David Smith and Michael Timberlake on passenger travel between world cities. In an earlier study, Smith and Timberlake analyzed data on the number of passengers traveling between pairs of 23 of the 30 world cites identified by John Friedmann in the 1980s. Their first finding was a high degree of connectiv-ity between all these world centers. The more important finding, however, was that more central nodes like New York, London, and Tokyo in the sys-tem have much heavier traffic flows to many more world cities than the less central cities. Paris turned out to score surprisingly high as a central node below London but above New York. In a more recent and refined analysis focusing on airline passengers among a much larger number of cities in Asia, Shin and Timberlake found what they termed cliques in which city mem-bers are relatively similar in terms of the volume of mutual airline passenger traffic. The two scholars also detected the shifting "centrality" of major Asian cities over time based on their similarities in the pattern of airline passenger flows to all other cities.[62]

As we have indicated, global perspectives on the city and their typical ana-lytic approaches fall into two distinctive categories, with some underlying conceptual overlaps between them. Together they have advanced the study of the city beyond the traditional premise of the city being a local unit shaped by its immediate regional context and by the territorial state it belongs to. A critical and yet balanced evaluation of either type of global perspective on the city will lead a better theoretical understanding of the local and extra-local dynamics that are transforming the city.

STRENGTHS AND WEAKNESS

The primary strength of the global perspective is that it offers a fresh viewpoint on the broader context in which the city exists and changes. From the world city hypothesis of Friedmann in the 1980s to Sassen's global city perspective in the 1990s, economic globalization accelerated and unleashed several powerful trends such as the much more rapid cross-border flow of financial capital and the development of new information technologies. These forces have propelled a few dominant international cities to the top of the global economic and urban hierarchy as global cites, while shaping other cities into more differentiated roles and positions. Scholars like John Friedmann and Saskia Sassen have alerted students of the city to see and appreciate the real impact of these external forces on the city. Armed with this global perspective, we should be in a stronger position to examine and understand how the global forces play out in the specific context of a city. The world city system perspective typified by David Smith and Michael Timberlake has provided an alternative conceptualization of the relational and systemic attributes of major cities in a global hierarchy. They also have introduced a more rigorous analytic approach to taking advantage of the available data on international transportation ties among cities. Their empirical contribution lies in mapping out some of these ties in such a way for students to see that cities indeed are related to one another in a hierarchical structure.

One major weakness of the global city perspective may be that its theorizing and analysis are based primarily on a few dominant and heavily studied cities in Western industrialized countries. One could question the explanatory power of this perspective for emerging global cities in the national context of industrializing developing countries. While there is a growing body of research on emerging world cities in non-Western countries, especially in the Asia-Pacific region, [63] it needs to be done with an eye toward evaluating the validity of Sassen's global city perspective. Despite the elegant conceptualization and analytic approach of the world city system perspective, it tends to be somewhat abstract and lacks the attention to the rich contextual qualities of the city. In addition, its empirical analysis is technically demanding and often constrained by limited data on the network attributes of cities. It therefore poses a strong analytic challenge to students who want to use it.

Conclusion

As you can tell, there are important differences among these alternative perspectives on the nature of the city. How one chooses to view the city will depend, in part, on what features of the city one wishes to emphasize. If one wishes to see the city through the eyes of its visual and cultural elements, then clearly one will draw heavily on the insights of writers like Zukin and Davis to draw a portrait of urban space. However, if one wishes to emphasize the recent impact of the global economy on cities, then clearly one would wish to draw on the insights and writings of figures like Sassen and Friedmann.

No one of these views is necessarily more correct than another. Indeed, the abundance of perspectives underscores the great richness of city and urban life, in general. We commend you to consider them carefully. Most importantly, we commend them to you as vantage points on the urban world, as ways that you can gain insight into how this world works and, armed with such knowledge, how you can gain a deeper appreciation of the world we now live in.

Notes

1 An excellent history of the Chicago school is to be found in Martin Bulmer, *The Chicago School of Sociology*. (Chicago: University of Chicago Press, 1984). Also see the recent history by Andrew Abbott, *Department and Discipline: Sociology at One Hundred* (Chicago: University of Chicago Press, 1999).

2 On Robert Park and Louis Wirth, see the appropriate biographical entries in Neil Larry Shumsky, editor, *The Encyclopedia of Urban America: The Cities and Suburbs* (Santa Barbara, California: ABC-Clio Publishers, 1998), pp. 553–4 and 880–1.

3 For a discussion of these various studies, see Bulmer, *Chicago School*, chapter 8.

4 For an array of various critiques of this research, see George A. Theodorson, ed., *Studies in Human Ecology*, Part I, Section B (Evanston, Illinois: Row, Peterson & Co., 1961).

5 On Park's broad view of these matters and sociology, more generally, see Robert E. Park, and Ernest W. Burgess, *Introduction to the Science of Sociology* (Chicago: University of Chicago Press, 1924).

6 Thomas S. Kuhn, *The Structure of Scientific Revolutions* (Chicago: University of Chicago Press, 1962).

7 Robert E. Park, "Human Ecology," *American Journal of Sociology*, 43 (July 1936) 1–15. For a short appraisal of this particular view, see Orum, "Urban Ecology," pp. 817–18 in Shumsky, ed., *The Encyclopedia of Urban America*.

8 Park and Burgess, *Introduction to the Science of Sociology*.

9 Ernest W. Burgess, "The Growth of the City: An Introduction to a Research Project," pp. 47–62 in Robert E. Park, Ernest W. Burgess, and R. D. McKenzie, ed., *The City* (Chicago: University of Chicago Press, 1925).

10 See, for example, Clifford R. Shaw, *The Jack-Roller: A Delinquent Boy's Own Story* (Chicago: University of Chicago Press, 1930).

11 Louis Wirth, "Urbanism as a Way of Life," *American Journal of Sociology*, 44 (January 1938): 1–24.

12 Georg Simmel, "The Metropolis and Mental Life," pp. 409–24 in Kurt Wolff, ed., *The Sociology of Georg Simmel* (Glencoe, Illinois: The Free Press, 1950).

13 Robert McKenzie, "The Concept of Dominance and World Organization," *American Journal of Sociology*, 33 (1927): 28–42. For a sharp critique of human ecology, see David A. Smith and Michael Timberlake, "World Cities: A Political Economy/Global Network Approach," pp. 181–207 in Ray Hutchison, ed., *Urban Sociology in Transition*. Research in Urban Sociology, Vol. 3, JAI Press, 1993.

14 Amos Hawley, *Human Ecology: A Theory of Community Structure* (New York: Ronald Press, 1950).

15 See also the general review of recent writings in human ecology, in W. Parker Frisbie and John D. Kasarda, "Spatial Processes," pp. 629–66 in Neil J. Smelser, ed., *Handbook of Sociology* (Newbury Park, California: Sage Publishers, 1988).

16 Walter Firey, "Sentiment and Symbolism as Ecological Variables," *American Sociological Review*, 10 (April 1945): 140–8.

17 In French, among others, see *La droit a la ville* (Paris: Anthropos, 1968; and *La Production de l'espace* (Paris: Anthropos, 1974). Recent English translations include *The Production of Space*. trans Donald Nicholson-Smith (Oxford: Blackwell, 1991); and *Writings on Cities*, trans. Eleonore Kofman and Elizabeth Lebas (Oxford: Blackwell, 1996).

18 Karl Marx, "The Eighteenth Brumaire of Louis Bonaparte," pp. 594–617 in Robert C. Tucker, ed., *The Marx–Engels Reader*, second edition (New York: W.W. Norton, 1978).

19 *The Production of Space*, pp. 33 ff.

20 Ibid., p. 151.

21 Mark Gottdiener, *The Social Production of Urban Space*, 2nd edn. (Austin: University of Texas Press, 1994).

22 For one general and comprehensive discussion of Castells' early writings, see Peter Saunders, *Social Theory and the Urban Question*, ch. 5 and 6 (New York: Holmes and Meier, 1981). Also see Gottdiener, *The Social Production of Urban Space*, chapter 4.

23 Manuel Castells, *The Urban Question*, trans. Alan Sheridan (Cambridge, Mass.: MIT, 1977). The original version is *La Question Urbaine* (Paris: Francois Maspero, 1972).

24 Manuel Castells, *The City and the Grassroots* (Berkeley: University of California Press, 1983).

25 Castells, *The Urban Question*, p. 21.

26 See his most recent ambitious efforts: *The Information Age: Economy, Society and Culture* (three volumes) (Oxford: Blackwell Publishers, 1997–9); and *The Rise of the Network Society*, 2nd Edn. (Oxford: Blackwell Publishers, 2000).

27 David Harvey, *Social Justice and the City* (Oxford: Basil Blackwell, 1973; 1988 reissued).

28 Ibid., p. 17.

29 Among other works by Harvey see *The Limits to Capital* (Oxford: Basil Blackwell, 1982); *The Urbanization of Capital* (Baltimore: Johns Hopkins University Press, 1985); *The Urban Experience* (Baltimore: Johns Hopkins University Press, 1989); *The Condition of Postmodernity* (Oxford: Blackwell, 1990).

30 Harvey, *Social Justice and the City*, ch. 5.

31 Harvey, *The Urbanization of Capital*, ch. 3.

32 See, for example, John Logan and Harvey Molotch, *Urban Fortunes: Toward a Political Economy of Place*. Berkeley: University of California Press, 1987).

33 Harvey, *The Urbanization of Capital*, ch. 1.

34 Also see Gottdiener, *The Social Production of Space*; and Mark Gottdiener and Joe R. Feagin, "The Paradigm Shift in Urban Sociology," *Urban Affairs Quarterly*, 24 (December 1988): 163–87.

35 *The Urban Experience*, chs. 4 and 5. Also see on the same general topic, Susan S. Fainstein, Ian Gordon and Michael Harloe, eds., *Divided Cities: New York and London in the Contemporary World* (Oxford: Blackwell, 1992); and John Mollenkopf and Manuel Castells, eds., *Dual City: Restructuring New York*. New York: Russell Sage, 1991.

36 Robert A. Dahl, *Who Governs?* (New Haven, Conn.: Yale University Press, 1961). Also see the lengthy discussion of Dahl, his view and influence, in Anthony Orum, *Introduction to Political Sociology*, 4th edn. (Englewood Cliffs, New Jersey: Prentice-Hall, Inc., 2000), ch. 7.

37 Harvey Molotch, "The City as a Growth Machine," *American Journal of Sociology*, 82 (September 1976): 309–32.

38 For an extended assessment of the research inspired by Molotch's argument, see John Logan, Rachel Bridges Whaley, and Kyle Crowder, "The Character and Consequences of Growth Regimes: An Assessment of 20 Years of Research, *Urban Affairs Review*, 32, 5 (May 1997): 603–30.

39 John Logan and Harvey Molotch, *Urban Fortunes: Toward a Political Economy of Place*.

40 See, e.g., Frisbie and Kasarda, "Spatial Processes."

41 Sharon Zukin, *Loft Living: Culture and Capital in Urban Change* (New Brunswick, New Jersey: Rutgers University Press, 1989); *Landscapes of Power* (Berkeley: University of California Press, 1991); and *The Cultures of Cities* (Oxford: Blackwell, 1995).

42 *Landscapes of Power*, ch. 8; *Cultures of Cities*, ch. 2.

43 Mike Davis, *City of Quartz: Excavating the Future in Los Angeles* (New York: Vintage, 1992).

44 Also see Harvey, *The Condition of Postmodernity*.

45 Kenneth T. Jackson, *Crabgrass Frontier: The Suburbanization of the United States* (New York: Oxford University Press, 1985).

46 Erik Monkonnen, *America Becomes Urban: the Development of United States Cities and Towns, 1780–1980* (Berkeley: University of California Press, 1988).

47 Anthony M. Orum, *City-Building in America* (Boulder, Co.: Westview Press, 1995).

48 Peter Hall, *The World Cities*, 3rd edn. (London: Weidenfeld and Nicolson, 1984).

49 John Friedmann and Goetz Wolff, "World City Formation: An Agenda for Research," *International Journal of Urban and Regional Research*, 6 (1982): 304–44; John Friedmann, "The World City Hypothesis," *Development and Change*, 17 (1986): 69–83.

50 Saskia Sassen, *The Global City: New York, London, Tokyo* 2nd edn. (Princeton, New Jersey: Princeton University Press, 2001).

51 Ibid., 3–4.

52 Ibid., chs. 5 and 6.
53 See Saskia Sassen, *Cities in a World Economy*, 2nd edn. (Thousand Oaks, California: Pine Forge Press, 2000); Sassen, ed., *Global Networks, Linked Cities* (New York and London: Routledge, 2002).
54 Sassen, *The Global City*, chs. 8 and 9; Sassen, *Cities in a World Economy*, chs. 3 and 6.
55 For another illustrative example of this global perspective, see James N. Rosenau, *Along the Domestic–Foreign Frontier: Exploring Governance in a Turbulent World* (New York Cambridge University Press, 1997).
56 Saskia Sassen, "New Frontier Facing Urban Sociology at the Millenium," *British Journal of Sociology*, 51 (January/March 2000): 146; also see her *Losing Control? Sovereignty in an Age of Globalization*. (New York: Columbia University Press, 1996).
57 See Ash Amin and Nigel Thrift, "Living in the Global," pp. 1–22 in Ash Amin and Nigel Thrift, eds., *Globalization, Institutions and Regional Development in Europe* (Oxford: Oxford University Press, 1994), p. 6; Philip McMichael, "Globalization: Myth and Realities," *Rural Sociology*, 61 (1996), 25–55.
58 For a diverse set of case studies of both United States and international cities from a global perspective, see "Globalization and the Changing U.S. City," David Wilson, special editor, *The Annals of the American Academy of Political and Social Science*, 551 (May 1997); Peter Marcuse and Ronald Van Kempen, eds., *Globalizing Cities: A New Spatial Order* (Oxford: Blackwell Publishers, 2000. For suggested politics for United States cities to compete in the global economy, see Dennis A. Rondinelli, James H. Johnson, Jr., and John D. Kasarda, "The Changing Forces of Urban Economic Development: Globalization and City Competitiveness in the 21st Century," *Cityscape: A Journal of Policy and Development Research*, 3 (1998): 71–105.
59 See Immanuel Wallerstein, *The Capitalist World-Economy* (Cambridge: Cambridge University Press, 1979).
60 See Smith and Timberlake, "World Cities." Also see the collection of essays in Paul Knox and Peter Taylor, eds., *World Cities in a World-System* (New York: Cambridge University Press, 1995).
61 David A. Smith and Michael Timberlake, "Conceptualizing and Mapping the Structure of the World System's City System," *Urban Studies*, 32, 2 (1995): 287–302.
62 Smith and Timberlake, ibid., p. 297; K. H. Shin and Michael Timberlake, "World Cities in Asia: Cliques, Centrality and Connectedness," *Urban Studies*, 37, 12 (2000): 2257–85.
63 See Fu-chen Lo and Yue-man Yeung, eds., *Emerging World Cities in Pacific Asia* (Tokyo: University Nations Press, 1996).

Social Inequalities and the Creation of Metropolitan Space

Social inequality is deeply associated with the emergence of cities and with the gradual creation of urban space over time. Where and how people live and work in the city are shaped by who they are and the resources they possess. What is especially interesting to observe is how these differences become embedded in the very terrain of the urban area – and how they also tend to be perpetuated over time, even though the landscape itself may change. Here in this chapter we want to consider how social inequalities come to shape the urban landscape over time, specifically, how social class, race and ethnicity, and gender – social differences of deep importance – become inscribed into the nature of urban spaces. We will illustrate these processes, in part, by drawing extensively on the history of urban growth in the United States.

Wealth and Power in the Creation of the American Metropolis

One of the inescapable facts about the nature of the modern city is how much its character has been shaped by the emergence and development of modern **capitalism.** Charles Tilly, a prominent sociologist, argues, for example, that the very emergence of the city in the modern West has been decisively shaped by the formation of capital.[1] As capital formations grew and became concentrated in specific sites, those sites themselves grew ever larger. Capitalism became the pivot around which populations would develop and cities emerge. Taking the same argument in a slightly different direction, the historian, Sam Bass Warner, Jr. argues that the forces of what he calls "**privatism**" have decisively shaped the construction of the city in America.[2] Privatism, or **capitalism**, shaped the very foundations of cities in America, from their emergence, in the seventeenth and eighteenth centuries, to their development over the course of time. To get a full sense of how decisive the role of capitalism has been in the construction of American urban areas, we begin our discussion with a look at the pre-industrial capitalist city.

THE PRE-INDUSTRIAL CAPITALIST CITY

The pre-industrial city was very different from the one we know today.[3] In terms simply of territory, it was much smaller and more compact. It was a place that could easily be traversed, what Warner refers to as a "walking city." Its population also was much smaller than that of today's cities, numbering generally on the order of tens of thousands, at most. But even though smaller, it was in some ways very similar to today's cities. Wealth and power, in particular, still left a very deep imprint on the shape of the pre-industrial city.

People of privilege were able to locate themselves at the center of the city. They ran their businesses from the center and lived in the most privileged places. In places like Philadelphia, or New York, for example, special quarters were set aside for the wealthy: there quarters comprised squares or other lovely residential areas, that had the most handsome and largest residences for the wealthy. People who were poor, in contrast, were confined to living in the more desolate and decrepit areas of the city. Often such areas were the outskirts of the city, places somewhat distant from the places of work.[4]

The center of government and power also occurred at the spatial center of the city. Often the richest and most influential business figures became the leaders of government as well. They were the first mayors of cities, and generally exercised power in such a way as to ensure that the wealthy would retain their privileges. In cities like Chicago, moreover, the business owners and the propertied class – that is the rich – were able to fashion rules that would serve to their advantage. Businessmen, for example, in Chicago helped to fashion rules that gave them special access to the sidewalks and pavements in the city, and made sure that their business would continue to operate successfully.[5] Moreover, long before monies had been set aside for governments to fashion urban areas, the wealthiest individuals also would pay for new roads and sidewalks – not, mind you, out of a strong sense of *noblesse oblige*, but because such streets and walks would make sure that their goods could get to market, and that people could get to their stores for business.[6]

Even in the smaller towns, well away from the route of the largest concentrations of people, the privilege of wealth and the disadvantage of poverty would make themselves felt deeply on the village landscape. In small cities, like Muncie, Indiana, for example, the wealthy families lived apart from the poor and working-class.[7] They lived in the privileged sections of town, often on hills overlooking the commerce and industry of the everyday city. By contrast, the poorer citizens of small towns were confined to living in less advantaged quarters, often near the center of town, or near waterfront areas. The privilege of class made itself felt early and often in the cities, firstly, by taking advantage for the sake of business of living in the center of town, and secondly, by appropriating the more desirable sites for their own living quarters.[8]

THE INDUSTRIAL CAPITALIST CITY

Once the industrial revolution occurred, roughly around mid-nineteenth century in America, it almost completely remade the social and physical landscape of the city. Industries tended to locate at the heart of the city, often because it was there that the transportation routes were the easiest, and access to goods and other commodities the quickest. Within a relatively short span of time, no more than a decade or so, the industrial revolution began to remake the nature of the economy of many cities, leaving in its wake not only new factories, to replace the smaller businesses of the pre-industrial era, but also new social classes.[9]

The factory became a window into the arrangements of the new social order of the city. Whether in leather or steel, bottle making or machines, the factory was the broad place where goods were assembled. Within it, there grew up sharp divisions between the workers, on the one hand, and the owners, and foremen, on the other. The workers were assembled at machines, toiling away, producing goods as speedily and efficiently as they could. Long before the advent of key labor laws, young children and women often toiled alongside men, creating many new implements to be sold in local markets or even abroad. The factory soon dominated the skyline of many central cities, creating an array of different smokestacks and plants in the downtown areas of many cities. It also became the hub of energy and industry for the city, promoting not only the growth of the local economy but also the growth of the city itself.

Because of political upheavals and declining economic opportunities in Europe, American cities, and their industries, soon drew in many immigrants from abroad, further reshaping the character of the American city. Jobs were quickly created, almost overnight, by the new plants and, as there were not enough domestic laborers to man the machines, workers were drawn into American cities from abroad. In places like Milwaukee, the new immigrants created a distinctively German cast to the city; so, too, a similar cast was

Plate 3.1   Steel works near Pittsburgh, 1909. Photo Lewis W. Hine. Courtesy George Eastman House.

created in cities like Cincinnati and St. Louis.[10] The new immigrants worked hard and long, helping the plants to churn out many new goods and creating a booming economy in the short space of one or two decades.

But the plants not only drew in immigrants and created new job opportunities, they also substantially reshaped the nature of the physical terrain of the city. Where once the skies had been crystal clear, and the atmosphere barely marked by small shops and craftsmen, now the machines and industry of this era began to spill out their refuse over the downtown areas of the city. Places like Buffalo, New York, or Chicago, Illinois, Milwaukee, or Pittsburgh, had skies that were rather quickly filled with refuse and soot, leaving their traces everywhere.[11] The refuse and spillage from the production lines made their way into local rivers; indeed a number of factories were located on such rivers to enable them both to take in and to ship out goods with ease. The rivers became deeply polluted, soiled by the refuse of plants and leaving deep streams of grime and dirt to run in the downtown areas.

Industry thus marked the new city, leaving not only massive profits but also refuse in its wake. The effect, of course, was to change and reshape the character of the industrial city, but to pose serious health threats to local citizens as well. The density of people living in the city, coupled with the use of privies and wells to carry human waste, invited the development and spread

Table 3.1   A historical time line chart for United States history

Date	Key Historical Events	Urban Developments
1860s	Beginning of Industrial Revolution in the US.	Industrial cities emerge.
1870–1900	Industries flourish. Eastern European immigrants enter America.	Cities expand greatly. Growth of working-class and immigrant settlements in cities.
1914–1918	World War I.	Beginning of Great Migration to the North. Growth of black communities in Chicago and Detroit. 1919 Rainbow Beach riot, Chicago.
1920s	Economic boom times in US.	Expansion of black communities in the North. Early growth of suburbs.
1930s	Great Depression.	Strikes in American cities. Growing unemployment.
1939–1945	World War II.	Incipient decline of urban infrastructures.
Late 1940s, early 1950s	War veterans return home.	Development of major interstate highway system. New suburban developments. Veterans move to new housing in suburbs; FHA support for home loans. Massive shifts of people begins to the Sunbelt states and cities.
1960s	Industries begin to move abroad and to the Sunbelt from North.	Loss of industrial jobs in northern cities. Incipient growth of the black underclass in urban areas such as Chicago,

		Detroit, Milwaukee. Population boom in Sunbelt cities, like Atlanta, Phoenix, Tucson, Orlando.
1965	1965 Hart–Celler Immigration Act.	By late 1960s a new generation of immigrants hits major American cities such as Houston, Miami and New York.
1970s and 1980s	Continuing loss of jobs overseas Recession in early and late 1980s	Severe economic problems hit some cities such as Cleveland and New York.
1980s–2000	Aging of the Baby Boomers Delay in marriage and in births by younger couples.	Growth in new residences in central cities. Rehabilitation of older industrial districts into new high-end residences.

of diseases among the new urban residents. Lacking vaccinations and anti-biotics, the creations of twentieth century medicine, illnesses spread quickly. Those who were most vulnerable to disease turned out to be the young and the elderly. But these diseases and the ills of the industrial age hit particu-larly hard at the workers and the working-class for they were the ones who often had to reside in the downtown areas, near the plants, there because they could not afford residences elsewhere. Soon, of course, tenements would arise in cities like Philadelphia and New York, or weak/shabby housing in cities like Milwaukee and Chicago. In Milwaukee, the workers were confined to living in the downtown areas, near the plants and thus more prey to the pollutants that spilled forth from them.[12]

At the same time as social differences were showing up on the floors of the factories so, too social differences were evident in the reshaping of the urban landscape. While the poor lived in the downtown areas, members of the wealthier classes often could live in the outlying areas. There tended to be a movement away from the central city among the very rich. In Chicago, the North Shore suburban areas developed in the late nineteenth century, places where the rich, like Julius Rosenwald, a co-founder of Sears could retreat on weekends and in the summers.[13] As forms of transportation became more readily available to places like Milwaukee or Pittsburgh, the wealthier classes

Plate 3.2   Blind beggar and poor children, 1911. Photo Lewis W. Hine. Courtesy George Eastman House.

of people, people who had grown rich as a result of the new industry, began to avail themselves of the more rustic areas nearby the downtowns, areas which could prove to be useful retreats both from the traffic of downtown and from the ill winds that often blew across the central cities.

THE EMERGENCE OF THE EARLY AMERICAN SUBURBS

rustic → 전원

The growth of **suburbs** is a phenomenon that predates the emergence of cities, at least in the United States. Suburban areas sprang up around English cities, for example, well before the industrial city took root there.[14] Such places generally were on the edges of the larger metropolitan areas, like London or Manchester, and seemed to have their roots as far back as the Middle Ages. They were small, rustic areas where the middle classes settled. In the late nineteenth century, such suburbs were carefully planned in England, towns and villages that were well designed, and were neatly set into the rustic landscapes.[15]

In America, too, the suburbs would develop, the result of an effort of Americans almost to seek, if not to reinvent, a bucolic past. Kenneth Jackson, Jr., the pre-eminent historian of the American suburbs, argues that such areas represented almost the ideal space for Americans – places where they could escape the hustle and bustle of city life, and yet achieve the privacy and property for which they seemed to yearn.[16] These kinds of suburban places arose in fairly large numbers, outside the urban areas, as early as the late nineteenth century. They were sought as a kind of refuge by the more wealthy citizens, places to which they could be transported by the rudimentary vehicles of transportation then available. This yearning for a private yard and a private place, Jackson argues, seems to lie deep in the psyche of Americans, a deep cultural ideal where both privacy and private property come together.[17]

By the turn of the century, these utopian venues came to surround most large urban centers in the United States. Gradually they grew in size, until the numbers of their occupants were in the hundreds, if not thousands. Moreover, because of the nature of the various laws and statutes in America, these smaller suburban areas were able to secure protection against the encroachment of larger cities, becoming incorporated as villages or towns, and thus able to create their own kind of self-government. In places like Milwaukee, these suburban areas arose all over, housing generally a wealthier population than those people who resided in the cities. Moreover, over time the suburban areas grew even farther apart than merely in terms of wealth. As cities grew larger in the early part of the twentieth century, many of them sought to incorporate their outlying suburban areas. By doing so, they would have relieved some of the population pressures they suffered, but also been able to secure monies that now went into the coffers of small towns and villages for their own protection.

Indeed, there grew to be great political differences between the suburban areas and the major urban centers, ones that mirrored their differences of wealth and social class. The cities could exercise great political clout, but generally were unable to draw in the suburban areas, largely because the political integrity of those areas were protected by state laws and because local residents often were unwilling to vote to become annexed to the nearby cities. Moreover, when cases came before state courts, the courts often ruled on behalf of the smaller localities, in part because the courts reflected the dominance of rural interests. The net result, then, in a number of metropolitan areas, was to create a kind of suburban ring around the urban center: the suburbs, consisting largely of wealthier citizens, refused to join with the municipal or other interests of the cities, and thus became like another jurisdiction altogether.[18] This kind of rock solid division first took root in St. Louis, and was marked by a famous judicial ruling that said, in effect, such divisions between suburbs and cities were legal. The ruling in 1875 subsequently set the course and tone for a whole set of American cities, putting into stone a kind of legislative barrier that came to protect the interests of the suburbs, and their wealthier residents, against those of the urban poor.

THE POST-INDUSTRIAL CITY

Although many industries began to depart the industrial cities of Northeastern and Midwestern America by the 1930s, spurred on by the ravages of the Great Depression, it was not until the early 1960s that many industries began to leave such cities in great droves. There were many reasons prompting their departure. For one thing, great splits had grown up between the unions and management in such cities, the legacy of several decades of conflict and fights over fair benefits and wages. In cities like Milwaukee or Detroit, the gap between the unions and management grew very wide, eventually leading some industries to pull up their stakes altogether.[19] For another thing, the lure of the South in the United States, or even of overseas manufacturing, was inescapable. The South was virtually without unions, thus making it possible for industries there to gain greater profits for themselves. Plants like Schlitz left Milwaukee for states like Texas precisely because there were no unions to fight with them on wages and benefits. Finally, in the post-World War II period, it now became much more possible for people to gain a satisfactory lifestyle in the Southern states. Air-conditioning, though seemingly a trivial invention, now became widespread through the South, making it much easier to live for those recently moved in from the North. Housing was cheaper as well in the South, and became a very attractive lure for new residents. Finally, there were states like Florida and California that soon became the haven of the aging who wished to escape the ravages of the northern climates.

Cities of the North

Such vast migration proved devastating to Northern cities in the period after the War. Tens of thousands of jobs were lost in manufacturing to such cities. The consequences were almost immediate and felt very deeply. A large sector of the labor force was left unemployed, many of whom were still in their 40s and 50s and fully capable of continuing to work for at least another ten years or so. The loss of wages and tax monies to the economy of the industrial cities of the North was also substantial. It meant, for example, that the physical infrastructure of the city now suffered greatly: roads could not be repaired, nor could bridges. Moreover, as more and more people left the central cities for the suburbs, the economic woes of the central cities increased greatly. Eventually a number of cities came close to bankruptcy; some like Cleveland and New York actually had to declare bankruptcy.[20]

The movement to the suburbs accelerated considerably in the post-World War II period. It was aided by a number of important factors, as the seminal analysis of Kenneth Jackson shows.[21] One of the key elements to the movement was the availability of low-interest loans to veterans, enabling them to purchase new homes in the suburbs at a fairly low cost. In addition, the interstate highway system, which had been designed and implemented just after the war, now made it possible for more and more citizens to leave the city for the suburbs, and yet for their wage-earners to return to the city for work.[22] Altogether, the movement from the central cities exacerbated the growing division of wealth and income between city and suburbs, a division that had first appeared much earlier in the century. Suburbs now blossomed, protected by various state laws. Because property taxes provided the bulk of monies for schools in the suburbs, schooling there also improved, while that available to the children in the central city declined almost proportionately.

The loss of manufacturing and the movement to the suburbs were two of the key factors that in the post-industrial cities of the North drove a further wedge between cities and suburbs, and a deeper wedge between the wealthier and poorer citizens. The poorer families simply could not afford to leave the cities easily, in part because they had to be close to their workplaces. The richer families, which now owned at least one if not two cars could make the trip easily to the suburbs and enjoy the various pleasures thereby obtained. In addition, there was a changing political complexion to the suburbs and the cities: the suburbs increasingly became home to the Republican Party, while the cities were left as Democratic strongholds. The social divisions, in other words, were inscribed on the metropolitan terrain, and across them were laid political differences that only served to reinforce them.

Cities of the Sunbelt

The story of post-industrial cities was quite different in the Southern United States, that area which became known as the Sunbelt. Here there were booming numbers of people. Although adding to the woes of state and local governments as efforts were made to increase roads and improve schools, furnish housing and build new businesses, the overall effect was to make the economies of these areas boom. In the period after World War II, the various population maps show clearly how there was a shift of balance in the population from the North to the South, from the Snowbelt to the Sunbelt.[23]

Here, in cities like Atlanta, Georgia, or Charleston, South Carolina, Dallas, Texas, or Phoenix, Arizona, there was a virtual boom in every sector of the economy.[24] Important lessons had been learned from the growth of Northern cities – particularly the lesson that it was essential to avoid the fractiousness of fights between cities and suburbs. Thus, cities like Phoenix and Tucson managed to grow enormously, partly because areas surrounding Phoenix were annexed long before any political divisions could be created.[25] Moreover, cities of the South were more apt to exercise home-rule than those of the North, meaning that such cities could indeed exercise much more political authority over their environs than Northern cities had been able to. In addition, the economy of the South had a special edge in the post-War period, having had many defense industries and plants built there during the war. States like Texas and California especially benefited from the largesse of the defense industry, partly because their Congressional representatives proved so effective at garnering such funds. There was a virtual makeover in the nature, then, of the US economy, wealth moving from the North to the South, alongside and parallel to that of the movement of population.

One of the most central features of the Southern post-industrial cities that was so key to their ability to move forward in the 1960s, 1970s and beyond was that many had been created by their founders and leaders to be precisely unlike the Northern industrial cities.[26] Tenements were thought to be a terrible legacy of the industrial revolution and poverty in the North, as was the polluted air. Thus efforts had been made, well in advance of the coming of people, to create a kind of city that would prove to provide all the right resources for building what would eventually become the "new economies" of the post-industrial age. Because cities and suburbs were not split as in the North, and because tenements had never been allowed to grow and house a great working class, for these and other reasons the deep class differences of the Northern industrial, and post-industrial, cities would not blemish the Southern landscape. However, poverty did exist and it would mark the landscape of the Southern city, poverty particularly among the minority groups. And that is the matter to which we shall now turn.

Race and Ethnicity in the Construction of the American Metropolis

Poverty and race, or poverty and ethnicity, are two phenomena that have become intertwined with one another in explaining the life chances of people, especially in the United States but in other nations as well. Often it is difficult to disentangle the effects of one, say wealth, from the other, say race. Often there are heated disagreements, as we shall soon see, between equally good social scientists about whether race or wealth matters more to a person's life chances. And yet, however much they are intertwined, it is important to consider them as separate analytical categories. Race, for example, has powerful effects on a person's life chances, above and beyond merely his, or her, wealth. Blacks and whites of similar education, for example, are apt today to be paid much differently for much the same kind of work.[27]

Here in this section we want therefore to consider the issues of race and ethnicity, and their impact on the metropolitan landscape. We shall consider them separately for, as will become clear, the issues that have faced African-Americans, as they have migrated from rural to urban areas, are very different from those that have influenced virtually every other minority group in American history.

The history of African-Americans in the United States is one that dates back to the early years of the seventeenth century. It was then that black Africans first were brought to the United States.[28] Most, if not all, had been kidnapped and absconded from their villages and homes in African nations, and brought unwillingly to the new lands of the Americas. The journey was often treacherous, resulting in the deaths of hundred of innocent blacks aboard the slave ships. But the journey was nothing compared to the conditions of slavery that the black Africans experienced once they arrived in the United States. For the next two centuries, black Africans were an enslaved population of people in America, working on plantations for white slave-owners under conditions that would test both their physical endurance and their humanity. Over time, the black Africans were turned into African-Americans, a population of unwilling immigrants whose experience would match no other in American history, save that of the original, native Americans.[29]

By the time that the slaves were freed in the 1860s, they had become a large, yet deeply scarred population, a group of people only too anxious to be freed from the plantations. Many made their way into the small towns and villages of the South, as did a few who had managed to escape to the North. In the earliest years of their freedom, the 1860s and 1870s, many blacks, lacking the financial and material resources necessary to survive in the more populated areas, became employees as domestics and servants for the urban population. Often the black families would live in separate quarters from whites, but, in these earliest years, there was little evidence of spatial separation between the two races. Research on Southern cities, like Atlanta and New Orleans in the period of Reconstruction, shows very little evidence of **segregation**. Indeed, there was more evidence of separate living areas for blacks and whites in the cities of the North than in those of the South.[30]

Creating segregation

Yet all that would soon change. The dominant Southern plantation owners, though they lacked the authority of the laws and traditions of slavery, were able to reinstitute a system of dominance to replace it, namely that of the Jim Crow laws.[31] These laws claimed simply that black Americans had no rights as citizens, and that they were to live apart in separate circumstances and quarters from whites. Jim Crow laws meant that black citizens could not hold the same jobs as whites, nor could they conduct business in the same quarters as whites. They were soon deprived of their brief tenure as citizens, becoming, in effect, second-class citizens who lacked the right to vote and to exercise the democratic franchise. Throughout the South especially, and in urban areas as well as in rural ones, the Jim Crow laws became dominant. The brief and temporary experience of integration, of living more or less alongside whites in urban areas, even though acting as their servants quickly gave way to a new form of slavery, one that created separate social, economic and spatial quarters for the African-Americans.[32]

Another blow to the efforts of African-Americans to enjoy real freedoms in the United States in the post-bellum period came in the decisive ruling by the Supreme Court in 1896. A case had been brought by a black litigant, Plessy, against the East Louisiana Railway, maintaining that he should be able to travel in the same railroad accommodations as white passengers. The Supreme Court, however, ruled in favor of the railroad, establishing a precedent for "separate but equal" facilities for blacks and whites that would stand for more than half a century. The result of the ruling was to create two classes of Americans, one that could enjoy all the freedoms that American democracy entitled them to as well as all the financial benefits they could create through harvesting their energies in nascent industrial capitalism. The other group, blacks, now became stripped of all rights – civil, political, social, and economic. Slavery had been resurrected but subtly transformed into segregation of the races. This left a mark on all institutions, but most especially on the urban landscape.

The great migration to the North

By the early part of the twentieth century, the conditions of Southern agriculture had begun to change in dramatic fashion. No longer able to compete successfully in the world markets of cotton and corn, many Southern plantations began to decline. At the same time, the growth of industries in the North made urban areas like Detroit and Chicago all the more attractive to people, especially the poor whites and blacks who lived in Southern rural areas. Beginning in the 1920s and 1930s, a massive shift of people began from the South to the North, most of whom were African-American migrants. The shift of blacks northward soon became known as the Great Migration. And it would leave a lasting impact on many Northern cities.[33]

Because of the growth of the automobile industry in Detroit, that city soon became a haven for many black migrants from the South. They quickly moved into areas nearby the auto plants and established new living quarters for themselves. Because of the prevalence of segregation in local housing practices, blacks were forced to move to areas where other blacks already lived, and thus far apart from the residence of whites. Over the course of the first half of the twentieth century, the black population of Detroit grew enormously, from one of 24,000 in 1920 to one of 352,000 in 1930.[34] The influx of so many new black residents was not without its serious side effects. In Detroit, for example, violent street clashes between the races broke out in the 1920s, the result of a growing conflict over housing and, especially, jobs between blacks and whites. In Chicago in 1919, a similar riot broke out, the so-called Rainbow Beach riot, that resulted in a number of deaths and injuries. Both sets of riots revealed the impact that the shift of so many black migrants had on Northern urban areas, and the tensions that resulted over issues like employment between whites and blacks.

Many other cities experienced the same as Detroit. Cleveland, for example, also soon became home to a large black population that, like Detroit, was segregated from the white residential areas. Chicago, too, witnessed the growth of its population of African-Americans. Over the course of the 1920s and 1930s, the black population soon came to take up residence on the South side of Chicago, particularly in the area along State Street south of the Loop. Within a short space of time, this area of the city became heavily populated by African-Americans. In the 1940s, two social scientists, St. Clair Drake and Horace Cayton, undertook a massive and seminal study of this area of Chicago, identifying it as Chicago's "**Black Metropolis**."[35] It was an area filled with various kinds of residences and all sorts of small and new businesses. In addition, it became marked by a variety of new cultural and religious forms of expression. Many small churches opened their doors along the streets, becoming available to all forms of new worshippers. A variety of musical forms also accompanied the flight of blacks from the South, producing and reproducing in Chicago a form of the music that became known as the Blues.

The strengths of the growing black population in Northern cities, however, soon became offset by the weaknesses and barriers they encountered. Segregation again and again reared its ugly head, limiting both the kinds of work and the kinds of housing that the black population could secure. Employers often preferred to hire recent ethnic immigrants from abroad rather than to make jobs available to African-Americans. Again, in Chicago over the course of the 1940s and 1950s there were a variety of ways in which blacks found themselves limited to living in certain areas of the city, particularly on the South side. Real estate agents, for example, would not take blacks into certain white areas of Chicago, thereby reinforcing the general tendencies for segregation. In Detroit, white homeowners associations grew up, and took the offensive against black residents.[36] If black families happened to move into white areas, signs and sounds of hostility often would greet them. Their homes might be set ablaze, or signs of the KKK be set afire on their front lawns. Hostility and violence often were targeted against blacks who sought to move out of their segregated neighborhoods, thereby reinforcing a decades-old pattern. Moreover, the local police often were loath to identify and

redlining

isolate those white citizens who were responsible for attacks against the black newcomers.

It was in this period, during the 1940s and 1950s, when certain groups emerged to spearhead the drive to limit the opportunities for blacks and to confine them to specific areas of the city. The real estate industry, as a whole, became the leading edge of segregation in Northern cities, acting, in effect, to gain whatever advantage it could from the plight and poverty of the black population.[37] Not only would agents fail to take African-Americans into the more desirable residential areas of cities like Detroit or Chicago, but they also worked hard to profit from the changing conditions of residential neighborhoods. By fostering the transformation of certain residential areas from white to black ones, real estate agents could profit from such changes. Ultimately segregation became deeply embedded in the living patterns and areas of the urban North.[38]

The growing racial gap in cities and the debate over its causes

In those decades after World War II, when many veterans returned home from the victories abroad, the patterns of segregation and racism that so deeply etched the character of the urban North became, if anything, more marked. Actions by the federal government helped to further the process of segregation in the cities, though perhaps unintentionally. New public housing projects, which had been fashioned by the government in an effort to provide for the poor, especially the black poor, became yet another way in which the lives of blacks would become more deeply separated from those of whites. Although it had been the hope that the new public housing projects would provide but a temporary way station on the way to better housing and better jobs, for many black families they became nothing more than a pit of despair, a place where young lives would be lost and all hope abandoned.[39] At the same time, the federal government was making it easy for white veterans to obtain loans to purchase housing in the suburbs at a low cost, thus helping to fuel a process that would eventually enlarge into "white flight." Moreover, many of the areas to which the white residents were able to move were places that had building covenants stipulating that no black residents would be permitted to reside therein.[40]

Even the many victories secured by the civil rights revolution in America were unable to make much of a dent in the prospects for better and more equitable housing conditions for blacks in urban places. The civil rights revolution, led by the Reverend Martin Luther King, Jr., had, for example, resulted in the passage of the 1964 and 1965 Civil Rights Acts. These new policies meant that blacks could no longer be denied the privileges of an educational experience the equal to that of whites, nor denied the opportunity to eat in the same restaurants, nor denied the right to vote at the ballot box.

Many such victories were of substantial importance, leading, for example, to a higher representation of blacks in the United States Congress, more black mayors of American cities, and a much greater clout for blacks in the Democratic Party. Yet in many important ways the civil rights revolution left untouched the shape and character of the American metropolis itself. Blacks still lived in the poorer residential quarters of the city; they still lived in the segregated areas of Chicago's South Side, or the inner city of St. Louis; or the poorer sections of Cleveland and Detroit. In brief, the political victories seem not to have led to a corresponding and important transformation of urban places.

As industries began to leave the metropolis, especially the Northern metropolis, in the early 1960s, the impact on the black population seemed to be especially severe. Areas in which black residents lived, either in the public housing projects or in the segregated quarters of decaying black housing, appeared to worsen. The level of poverty among black families grew at rates that seemed far to exceed those of white families. Moreover, it became apparent that many black neighborhoods were suffering not merely from poor housing, but also from a growth in the amount of crime, the general level of gang activity, the increase in drug use and drug sales. High school drop out rates among black youth began to rise, and the rate of single-parent families also increased. These and other changes that worsened black neighborhoods set off a sometimes heated debate among social scientists over the causes of such decline, a debate that continues today and, for the most part, remains unresolved between the contesting sides.

One argument claims that the great gaps in economic accomplishments and wealth between blacks and whites can be traced to *the loss of jobs* that occurred to many Northern areas as a result of the loss of so many industries in the decades of the 1960s, 1970s and 1980s. This argument, which receives its most eloquent expression in the writings of sociologist William Julius Wilson, argues, in effect, that it is the loss of well-paying industrial jobs in urban centers, and their replacement with lower-paying opportunities, that has produced such a serious decline in the urban prospects and fortunes of African-Americans.[41] Wilson insists that there have been broad structural changes to the American economy, changes that, among other things, have sent the best manufacturing jobs overseas, produced a booming and broad new service industry, and resulted in many new economic opportunities and businesses, most of which are to be found in the suburban areas that ring the major cities. The result, in the words of sociologist John Kasarda is a "spatial mismatch"; in other words, the people who most need the new well-paying jobs – the African-Americans – are the most spatially removed in the city from those jobs, which now increase in numbers in the suburbs. Wilson also further insists that the civil rights revolution did have an important impact for the black population, but for the middle classes, not the poorer. It permitted more middle-class blacks to move into new suburbs – though often exclusively black suburbs – but thereby worsened the plight of the inner city black poor who now not only had no jobs, but had no role-models to emulate.

But sociologists Douglas Massey and Nancy Denton take issue with Wilson. Drawing on the long history of blacks and whites in American urban centers, they argue that it is not the loss of jobs, per se, that has produced the declines for urban blacks, but the ***continuing force of racial segregation*** in the cities.[42] Noting many of the facts we have already discussed here, Massey and Denton argue that, had it not been for the practices of residential segregation, many black families could have had the opportunity to improve their chances for success. Such families, Massey and Denton argue might have been able to secure new jobs had they only been able to move into the areas closer to where the new jobs are to be found. They observe that the impact of racial segregation is so powerful that, with the declines of industry that took place over the course of the 1970s and 1980s, it is segregation alone that could account for the growing impoverishment of the black population. Moreover, they also find, like many analysts, that there are many practices today that, despite federal legislation, strengthen rather than diminish the force of urban segregation. They include such practices as "redlining" by banks and lenders, a process which, in effect, says that certain areas of the city (identified by red lines) contain properties on which home loans and mortgages will not be made – and all such areas are the ones occupied by poor blacks or other minority groups.[43]

Today the argument continues unabated between those who insist the racial gap in material success is the result of the loss of old inner-city industry coupled with the growth of new suburban industry, on the one hand, and those who point to the continuing force of racial segregation, on the other. Some of the latest evidence in on this matter, in fact, suggests that both Wilson and Massey/Denton may be partly right. Lincoln Quillan, in an important recent piece of research, finds that both camps may be right. In particular, he discovers that since 1970 there has been a migration away of the middle-class away from moderately poor neighborhoods, creating pockets of high poverty, thus supporting the claims of Wilson. At the same time, however, he finds that while African-Americans have moved into predominately white neighborhoods, those same neighborhoods tend to lose white population rapidly, supporting the segregation thesis of Massey and Denton.[44] Nevertheless, whoever is right finally in this debate, the one fact that must not be obscured is this: the inequalities between blacks and whites persist, and they persist and are most deeply and variously etched in the landscape of metropolitan America. And it is the shape and contours of that landscape – the various laws, policies, and customs – that, until changed, will continue to leave racial inequality as a painful and lasting mark on American history.

The experience of European immigrants, especially those who entered the city during the course of the late nineteenth and early twentieth centuries, does not match that of African-Americans, mainly because most such immigrants entered the United States under entirely different circumstances, and at a time when many more employment opportunities existed. Although there is a wealth of material covering many of these immigrant groups, here we simply want to highlight some of their common experiences and show how they were associated with shaping the urban landscape.

Beginning late in the nineteenth century, tens of thousands of Europeans entered American cities. By the time the peak of such migration had concluded, in the 1930s, more than 14 million immigrants had resettled in the United States, soon to leave their own marks on the American soil. Because many such groups entered this country with few skills and material resources, they were compelled to join the long lines of people working in factories. Most, indeed, became members of the great urban working classes, manning the machines and turning out goods that, in the end, produced great profits for their employers. But, despite their common economic circumstances, each and every ethnic immigrant group ended up producing, or reproducing, its own special communities in the city.

Thus, for example, the Jews settled in certain specific areas of the city of Chicago, creating a new Jewish ghetto that resembled, in certain respects, the older ghettoes of Europe.[45] Jews started new businesses, and many quickly became quite wealthy overnight, even though they remained in the older Jewish quarters of urban America. Many Jews also settled in New York City at the end of the nineteenth century, creating what has now become legend in American urban history, the Lower East Side.[46] This became a beehive of activity and vitality for the Jewish community in America, a place where Jews could reside among others like themselves, and where they could easily establish new businesses and, on the Sabbath, walk to new temples or synagogues – places to worship that were so central to their lives. Although many Jews lived in poverty in the Lower East Side, the very nature of the community – the abundance of small businesses, of social opportunities, of political life – deeply shaped the character not only of Jews, but also of the city of New York.[47]

Other groups established their own special residential niches within different cities. In Chicago there was a very large Italian immigrant area, on the near West Side of the city. Again, it grew up, in part, because the places of work were located in the downtown area of the city, and thus within easy access to the Italian community. Moreover, the Italian community here became the site of one of the great social inventions of the American experience, Hull House, founded and operated by Jane Addams. Here Addams and

Plate 3.3 Boys in the street, New York City. Photo Lewis W. Hine. Courtesy George Eastman House.

her associates worked with the immigrants, helping to educate them and to provide them with the resources necessary to locate and secure new jobs. They developed a model for social welfare and immigrant services in the United States, as well as helping to fund and establish the first social scientific studies ever of the impact of the new immigrants on the American metropolis.

Many of these new immigrant communities looked very much the same. Immigrants often resettled with one another from the "Old Country," in effect recreating their old villages from Europe in the United States. Moreover, these ties between Europe and America worked as what have been called "immigration chains," furnishing broad and significant social networks of information and help, especially to Europeans who wanted to come to the United States. Often, too, the husband would come first, perhaps with his sons, and later, once having secured a job and livelihood in America, send for his wife and other children. Again these shifts in population helped to shape the character of urban America, creating centers of immigrant life here that in many ways resembled those from abroad. Each and every new immigrant place became a site where people not only could speak and do business with one another in the same language, but often may have known the people as friends and neighbors from Europe.

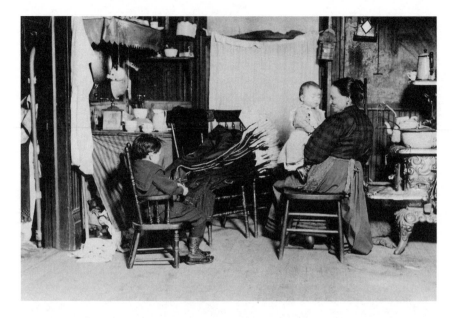

Plate 3.4   Interior of tenemant house. Jane Addams Memorial Collection (JAMC neg. 1002). The University Library, University of Illinois at Chicago.

Soon the American metropolis became a place of great and diverse ethnic flavors, a site where a variety of languages could be heard and where different cultures came in contact with one another. Moreover, because the European immigrants entered the United States when there was such a wealth of employment opportunities, drawn here, indeed, by the great industrial boom of the late nineteenth and early twentieth centuries, their experience was vastly different than that of African-Americans. Blacks moved to Detroit in the 1920s, or to Chicago about the same time, but they were unable to secure the kinds of jobs as European immigrants. Moreover, as shown above, they also faced barriers to opportunity unlike any of those faced by American blacks. Moreover, the European immigrants often were able to wield a degree of political power in urban areas unlike that of blacks. For example, in cities like New York, the Irish and the Italians were able to take over the reigns of Democratic Party power, in the form of Tammany Hall, thereby facilitating their eventual success in America, moving up both the political and the economic ladders of success.[48]

Over time, a pattern developed for the European wave of immigrants, one generally not found among African-Americans. It was a pattern that would be called "**assimilation**" by sociologists at the University of Chicago.[49] It meant, in effect, that over time, as a group of immigrants continued to live in

Plate 3.5   Market area near Hull House. Jane Addams Memorial Collection (JAMC neg. 313). The University Library, University of Illinois at Chicago.

the city and, especially, as their children and grandchildren were born in the city, they would tend to move to outlying suburban areas of the city, taking up residence in more prosperous residential settings. In effect, their spatial distribution in the metropolis mirrored that of their social and economic success: the more their education, the greater their wealth, the more likely the second- and third-generation immigrant family would move to the suburbs. This was a pattern repeated time and again. Second- and third-generation Jews, for example, moved from downtown Chicago to suburbs just north of the city, like Rogers Park, and eventually thereafter to even more exclusive and spatially removed suburbs, like Glencoe or Highland Park. Almost identical experiences happened to such immigrant groups as the Poles, the Italians, and the Irish. Yet, even with the spatial movement outward, many areas of the city retained their ethnic immigrant cast, remaining known as Old Polonia, Chinatown, and the Irish quarters.

In many cities today, signs from the European wave of immigrants can still be found, traces of an earlier history and a more difficult time. Marks of German immigrant influence still remain in Milwaukee, for example, evident in certain restaurants and cultural institutions in the downtown area. The same can be said of cities like St. Louis or of Cincinnati. Moreover, much of the culture that such groups brought with them have made their way into the American habits, creating a broader and richer variety of foods, of music and of literature. Still, the diversity and assimilation of this older generation of immigrants in the American metropolis occurred at a time much different than today – one of considerable job opportunities and of a wealth of fledgling institutions, like those of Tammany Hall, ready to absorb the newcomers. Today's urban immigrants face a different historical climate. And they come from origins much different than those of yesterday.

ETHNIC IMMIGRANTS: THE POST-1965 WAVE AND TODAY'S METROPOLIS

The first thing that must be noted about the current wave of immigrants to American shores is that they are very different from all previous generations. The 1965 Immigration Act basically transformed the character of immigration to the United States. First of all, it lifted the heavy restrictions that had been imposed on immigration in 1924 by the Congress. At that time, inspired by a period of xenophobia, the Congress moved to clamp down on all immigration from abroad. It put into effect various restrictions, both on the numbers and the country of origins of new immigrants. It established severe quotas on the numbers, thereby drastically reducing the flood of immigrants who entered between 1880 and 1924. In addition, it said that it would give preference to immigrants in proportion to their current numbers in the United States. That meant that those national groups already in the United States in heavy numbers, such as the English and the Germans, or, in general, the Western Europeans were heavily favored in the admissions criteria. The intent was to keep the national character of the United States pretty much as it was at the time.[50]

By the early 1960s, there was a heavy outcry that the standards for immigration were far too severe, and that, in particular, they made it difficult for political refugees from abroad, particularly from Southeast Asia, to enter the United States. Thus, in 1965 a new Act was put into effect, and the result has been both to dramatically increase the numbers of immigrants, and also to change fundamentally their national origins. Since that time, more than 20 million foreign-born people have taken up residence in the United States, a minority of whom now are naturalized citizens. Their distribution across metropolitan areas in many ways resembles that of the early generations, but there are also some key differences.[51]

Today's new immigrants, the majority of whom come from Latin American countries, such as El Salvador, Colombia, and Mexico, as well as from African nations, and from Asia, have targeted several key metropolitan areas as the places to which they migrate. The five largest entry points for the post-1965 generation are: Los Angeles, New York, Miami, San Francisco-Oakland, and the greater Chicago metropolitan area, including the stretch from Kenosha, Wisconsin to Gary, Indiana. They have helped these cities enormously, particularly by providing low-wage workers for local industries. The flood of recent immigrants to Los Angeles has been so profound that today the population of the city of Los Angeles consists of about four and one-half million foreign-born residents, or roughly 33 percent of the entire population. Los Angeles, in particular, has been reshaped by the waves of new immigrants.[52] Korean immigrants have established major new **enclaves** in portions of the city, and many have been enormously successful in recent decades in business, and in helping their children to achieve great success in American high schools and colleges. The Koreans simply have added to the distinctively Asian character long evident in the Los Angeles metropolitan region. Other cities in California, such as San Francisco, also are home to large groups of Asian residents, Chinese in particular, in the famed Chinatown area of the city.[53]

Their recent immigrant populations also have reshaped cities like New York and Miami. Miami, for example, witnessed a rapid influx of immigrants from Cuba just after the revolutionary takeover by Fidel Castro in 1959. The Cubans in Miami within a short space of time created a substantial ethnic enclave, one that, as recent research shows, provides a range of economic opportunities whose compensation outdoes that of employment opportunities outside the Cuban community.[54] In New York, by contrast, there are several Latino populations, chief among them the Central Americans, Salvadorans and the Puerto Ricans. Immigrants from Puerto Rico have been in New York for years, though their presence in recent years has diminished compared to other Latino populations. Moreover, they have created their own ethnic place, what has become known as "El Barrio." Like other recent immigrant enclaves, it has become populated by a poor and unemployed population, many of whom lost their jobs as industries left the city. On the other hand, the Salvadorans have been very successful in New York economic enterprises.[55]

In other words, the latest generation has created a number of its own ethnic niches and enclaves, sometimes replacing older groups that moved to the outlying areas. But there has also been something remarkably new about these immigrants. Many have bypassed the central city, once the first home to America's immigrants, and taken up residence in suburban areas. In Chicago, for example, recent Mexican immigrants can be found throughout the metropolitan area, ranging from the downtown to outlying suburbs. Many of these new communities have grown up rather quickly, their growth fueled by the continuing numbers of Mexicans who enter the United States each year. There are a number of studies now underway documenting the growth of such new immigrant communities throughout the American metropolitan area, and seeking to better explain why they have happened. In part, it now seems, the new enclaves have developed in older industrial areas, sites

immigrant experience compared in LA

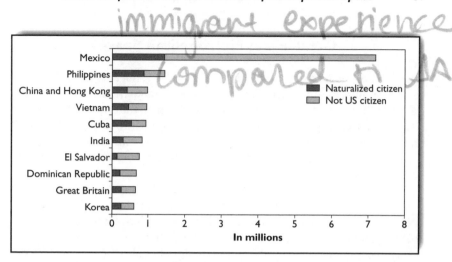

Figure 3.1   Foreign-born population by country of origin and citizenship status, 1999.

once occupied by the older, poorer generation of American immigrants who have since died off. But in other places, the new immigrant communities consist of people, often from Asia and India, who bring with them rich and varied skills, and who take up positions in the computer industry, in the pharmaceutical industry and in other high-paying forms of American industry. In other words, many of the new immigrants, particularly those with skills, are assuming the jobs that have cropped up in the outlying areas of the American metropolis, jobs that, because of the distance in part, are not accessible to African-Americans.

The recent American experience with immigrants, we must add, is not uncommon among nations today. Indeed a number of other nations, particularly in Europe, are witnessing similar flows of immigrants into them, and their metropolitan areas are changing dramatically as a result. London, for example, once only home to the native British and to members of the Commonwealth, has been flooded in recent years by growing numbers of immigrants from various parts of the world. So, too, Paris has become home to many new immigrants, as has Berlin. New enclaves have been developed in these metropolitan areas as well, producing various cultural and culinary imports. But the wave of new immigrants has also brought about its downside, too. In England, for example, many clashes and fights have broken out in recent years among different immigrant groups, especially those that live spatially proximate to one another in cities like London and Oldham. Our next chapter, on globalization and the city, will cover some of these matters in greater depth.

Gender and Metropolitan Space

Like race, ethnicity and social class, gender and gender relations have left their deep imprint on metropolitan space. Yet unlike these social inequalities and differences, the actual empirical research on the impact of gender on cities is relatively sparse. Indeed, it has only been within the past ten or fifteen years or so, that sociologists and geographers, among others, have turned their empirical lenses on the ways that gender becomes inscribed into spatial differences.

One of the first clues that set off researchers to the ways that gender might figure into the creation of metropolitan space sprang from the work of Michel Foucault.[56] Foucault argued that social institutions have a special history in shaping and disciplining human beings, and that such a history involves not simply mental representations and thought but also the way people conceive of their bodies.[57] The body, Foucault suggested, became something like a template on which the work of social institutions, like those dealing with issues of sexuality and gender, became emblazoned. To feminists, especially, this represented a powerful insight, providing a way to acknowledge how larger social institutions created gender and gender inequalities in prestige and power.

From notions of the body and of space, as we showed earlier in chapter 1 (see pp. 5–7), it then is a short step to examining the ways in which social institutions also help to manufacture the particular spaces set aside for men and women, that is, how they engender space. Many feminist scholars argue, for example, that the history of the West is not only the history of modern capitalism, but also the history of patriarchy and of the ways that men secure and retain their power over women. In a particularly apt illustration of the gendering of space, geographer Linda McDowell has created a set of binary oppositions that reveal the ways that we in the West have come to think of male and female spaces. Note in the list, shown here in table 3.2, that the home is thought of the female space and the workplace as the male space. These kinds of oppositions run throughout Western thought, owing their existence, as feminists point out, to the way that patriarchy has left its mark on Western society.

Sociologists have explored some of these differences in the engendering of space. The sociologist/urban planner, Daphne Spain, has accomplished the most detailed and exacting of this research. Spain has pursued two important lines of inquiry, one into a cross-cultural analysis of gender relations and space, and the other into the ways in which women's groups and organizations helped to create the American city in the late nineteenth and early twentieth centuries. In her first line of work, Spain proposed a simple hypothesis: where gender relations are such that males exercise more au-

Table 3.2   Masculine and feminine traits

The Masculine	The Feminine
Public	Private
Outside	Inside
Work	Home
Work	Leisure/Pleasure
Production	Consumption
Independence	Dependence
Power	Lack of Power

Source: Linda McDowell, *Gender, Identity & Place*, p. 13.

thority and power than females, there will more likely be separate and independent space set aside for men and women. In other words, where there is a kind of gender stratification system that favors males, then male power, in effect, will be transformed into separate quarters and spatial areas for men and women. "By controlling access to knowledge and resources through the control of space," Spain argues, "the dominant group's ability to retain and reinforce its position is enhanced. Thus, spatial boundaries contribute to the unequal status of women."[58] Spain tested her hypothesis by comparing various societies, from smaller, developing ones to more advanced societies, and by examining the distribution of space from special huts set aside in primitive societies to the distribution of space between men and women in the modern workplace. Generally, her findings supported her basis hypothesis: where the status and power differentials favored males, the gender differences in space were the greatest, evident everywhere from the smallest, most intimate spaces, like that of the home, to the largest, most public spaces, like that of separate educational spheres. Men, in brief, are able to exercise their authority and power over women in patriarchal societies by maintaining separate spaces for themselves, a fact that helps, Spain further explains, men retain their strict control over such key resources as knowledge and information.

In her latest work on the subject, Spain has examined the ways in which women's organizations at the turn of the twentieth century shaped the development of metropolitan space.[59] In particular, she studied four organizations – the Young Women's Christian Association (YWCA), the Salvation Army, the College Settlements Association and the National Association of Colored Women (NACW). She was especially interested in uncovering the ways that these organizations created what she calls "redemptive spaces," that is, spaces in the city created by women to provide comfort and shelter for the poor, the young, the infirm, and the newcomer from abroad. She finds

that the women's organizations performed important, but often unacknowledged, work in shaping the modern metropolis, particularly in terms of creating and shaping new spaces, such as playgrounds and nurseries for
children, or areas of public recreation like swimming pools and parks. Women
in the late nineteenth and early twentieth centuries in America, she notes,
created special areas of the city that provided shelter against the onslaught
of the ravages of industrialization, and, in so doing, left a mark on the city
certainly as important as the large and massive structures designed by men
such as Frank Lloyd Wright and Mies Van de Rohe. Moreover, by going to
great lengths to provide the documentary evidence of this history, Spain helps
to correct an obvious imbalance in how we think about metropolitan history, moving us from a history simply of buildings and plants, forged by men,
to one that acknowledges the vital work of women and their organizations
as well.

Research today on the engendering of metropolitan space is only in its
early stages, but it already has taken a number of interesting turns. For
example, there is a growing recognition of the ways that gays and lesbians
figure into the creation of metropolitan space. Years ago, the sociologist
Manuel Castells (see also chapter 2) noted that the Castro district of San
Francisco, where gay men came to predominate in the 1970s, was an area
both of vulnerability but also of power. Gay men, he suggested, exercised
their power, in part, by taking control of certain areas of the metropolis.[60]
More recent work on gay men and the metropolis, in Washington, D.C.,
suggests that the areas heavily populated by gay men are both areas of
power and of vulnerability. For example, while many gay men in Washington, D.C. have come to reside in the area of Dupont Circle, thus exercising control of it, it is in this same area that most of the violent attacks occur
against gay men.[61]

Much remains to be learned about how social institutions shape the metropolis in ways that affect the relations between men and women, and
gays/lesbians and heterosexuals. One of the more interesting questions to
consider is how the modern metropolis might look if the roles of men and
women had not only been equal, but also reversed. If, in other words, the
traditional caregivers in Western society had had more responsibility for
the creation of metropolitan space, might the space today work and look
very differently? Would public spaces, like parks, be as foreboding as they
are today? If women, as Spain suggests, had exercised even greater authority over the municipal housekeeping functions of the metropolis, might the
American metropolis be a more intimate and accessible place than it is today? No one has the answers, of course, but questions like these remain
deeply intriguing and require that we continue to accumulate evidence
about the ways in which the engendering of metropolitan space has historically taken place.

Conclusion

Just as Henri LeFebvre suggested, the creation of space plays a very important part in our lives as human beings. Nowhere is his basic insight more
powerful than in the ways that social differences, and social inequalities, become deeply imbedded in the workings of cities and suburbs. Capitalism and
social class have played an overarching role in the history of the American
city, with the privileges of wealth and upper-class being evident not only in
the structure of the workplace but also in the distribution of classes and resources across the metropolis: the poorer segments of the population inevitably are left to live in the worst areas of the city, while the wealthier have
the ability to move into the more expansive and costlier areas. Race and ethnicity have also left their mark, often independently of class. In recent times
especially, the inner city has become home to the black poor, in part because
of the powerful history and effects of racial segregation in America, in part
because the newer and higher-paying jobs have left the inner city for the
outer suburban areas. And finally, as the work of Daphne Spain shows, gender differences and relations are also inscribed into the creation of space in
societies: where the system of stratification favors the power and privilege of
males, there too the spatial differences and separation between males and
females is also the greatest. Gender privilege, in effect, seeks to protect itself
by maintaining spatial distance.

Notes

1   Charles Tilly, *Coercion, Capital and European States, AD 990–1990* (Cambridge, MA: Basil Blackwell Publishers, 1990).
2   Sam Bass Warner, Jr., *The Private City: Philadelphia in Three Periods of Its Growth* (Philadelphia: University of Pennsylvania Press, 1968).
3   Gideon Sjoberg, *The Preindustrial City, Past and Present* (Glencoe, IL: Free Press, 1960).
4   Ibid.
5   Robin Einhorn, *Property Rules: Political Economy of Chicago, 1833–1872* (Chicago: University of Chicago Press, 1991).
6   Anthony M. Orum, *City-Building in America* (Boulder, CO: Westview Press, 1995).
7   Robert S. and Helen Merrell Lynd, *Middletown in Transition: A Study in Cultural Conflicts* (New York: Harcourt, Brace, 1937).
8   W. Lloyd Warner, *The Social Life of a Modern Community* (New Haven: Yale University Press, 1947).
9   Bayrd Still, "Patterns of Mid-Nineteenth Century Urbanization in the Middle West," *Mississippi Valley Historical Review*, 28 (September 1984): 187–206.
10 Ibid.; Orum, *City-Building*.
11 Judith Walzer Leavitt, *The Healthiest City: Milwaukee and the Politics of Health*

Reform (Madison: University of Wisconsin Press, 1996), Martin V. Melosi, *The Sanitary City: Urban Infrastructure in America from Colonial Times to the Present* (Baltimore: The Johns Hopkins University Press, 2000).

12   Orum, *City-Building*.

13   Michael H. Ebner, *Creating Chicago's North Shore: A Suburban History* (Chicago: University of Chicago Press, 1988).

14   Kevin McDonnell, *Medieval London Suburbs* (London: Phillmore & Co., Ltd, 1978).

15   Carol Corden, *Planned Cities: New Towns in Britain and America* (Beverly Hills, CA: Sage Publishers, 1977); Alan Farmer, *Hampstead Heath* (New Barnet: Historical Publications, 1984); Mervyn Miller and A. Stuart Gray, *Hampstead Garden Suburb* (Sussex: Phillmore & Co., Ltd, 1992); and Roy Porter, *London: A Social History* (London: Hamish Hamilton, 1994), chapter 13.

16   Kenneth T. Jackson, *Crabgrass Frontier: The Suburbanization of the United States* (New York: Oxford University Press, 1986).

17   Robert Fishman, *Bourgeois Utopias: The Rise and Fall of Suburbia* (New York: Basic Books, 1987).

18   Jon Teaford, *City and Suburb: The Political Fragmentation of Metropolitan America, 1850–1970* (Baltimore: The Johns Hopkins University Press, 1979).

19   Orum, *City-Building*; Thomas Sugrue, *The Origins of the Urban Crisis: Race and Inequality in Postwar Detroit* (Princeton: Princeton University Press, 1995).

20   Paul Peterson, *City Limits*. Chicago: University of Chicago Press, 1981); Todd Swanstrom, *The Crisis of Growth Politics: Cleveland, Kucinich, and the Challenge of Urban Populism* (Philadelphia: Temple University Press, 1985).

21   Jackson, *Crabgrass Frontier*.

22   One of the best urban histories on these issues is that by Robert Fogelson on Los Angeles. Though it is considered a West Coast city, the case illustrates how highways came to shape and fuel the decentralization of people and, eventually, to add to the fragmented character of Los Angeles. Robert Fogelson, *The Fragmented Metropolis: Los Angeles, 1850–1930* (Berkeley: University of California Press, 1993). Also see Scott Bottles, *Los Angeles and the Automobile: The Making of the Modern City* (Berkeley: University of California Press, 1987).

23   Kirkpatrick Sale, *Power Shift: The Rise of the Southern Rim and Its Challenge to the Eastern Establishment* (New York: Random House, 1975); David C. Perry and Alfred J. Watkins, eds., *The Rise of Sunbelt Cities* (Beverly Hills, CA: Sage Publishers, 1977).

24   Richard M. Bernard and Bradley R. Rice, eds., *Sunbelt Cities: Politics and Growth Since World War II* (Austin, TX: University of Texas Press, 1983); Carl Abbott, *The New Urban America: Growth and Politics in Sunbelt Cities* (Chapel Hill, NC: University of North Carolina Press, 1987); Joe R. Feagin, *Free Enterprise City: Houston in Political and Economic Perspective* (New Brunswick, NJ: Rutgers University Press, 1988).

25   Bernard and Rice, Sunbelt Cities.

26   See, e.g., Anthony M. Orum, *Power, Money & The People: The Making of Modern Austin* (Austin, TX: Texas Monthly Press, 1987).

27   There is a voluminous literature on this topic. For some recent examples, see Andrew Hacker, *Two Nations: Black and White, Separate, Hostile, Unequal* (New York: Ballantine Books, 1992); and the many writings of Joe R. Feagin, includ-

ing Joe R. Feagin and Melvin P. Sikes, *Living with Racism: The Black Middle-Class Experience* (Boston: Beacon Press, 1994).

28 For an early and important anthology of writings on these matters, see Leslie H. Fishel, Jr. and Benjamin Quarles, *The Negro American: A Documentary History* (Chicago: Scott, Foresman Company, 1967).

29 John W. Blassingame, ed., *Slave Testimony: Two Centuries of Letters, Speeches, Interviews and Autobiographies* (Baton Rouge, LA: Louisiana State University Press, 1977); Stanley M. Elkins, *Slavery: A Problem in American Institutional and Intellectual Life* (Chicago: University of Chicago Press, 1976); Eugene D. Genovese, *Roll, Jordan, Roll: The World the Slaves Made* (New York: Pantheon Books, 1974); Kenneth M. Stampp, *The Peculiar Institution: Slavery in the Ante-Bellum South* (New York: Knopf, 1956); and Winthrop D. Jordan, *White Over Black: American Attitudes Toward the Negro, 1550–1812* (Chapel Hill, NC: University of North Carolina Press, 1968).

30 Leon F. Litwack, *North of Slavery: the Negro in the Free States, 1790–1860* (Chicago: University of Chicago Press, 1965).

31 C. Vann Woodward, *The Strange Career of Jim Crow* (New York: Oxford University Press, 1974).

32 For an example of the power of such laws in one Southern city, see Orum, *Power, Money & The People: The Making of Modern Austin*, ch. 7.

33 Nicholas Lemann, *The Promised Land: The Great Black Migration and How It Changed America* (New York: Vintage Books, 1992); James R. Grossman, *Land of Hope: Chicago, Black Southerners, and the Great Migration* (Chicago: University of Chicago Press, 1989).

34 Reynolds Farley, Sheldon Danziger, and Harry J. Holzer, *Detroit Divided* (New York: Russell Sage, 2000); Sugrue, *The Origins of the Urban Crisis*.

35 St. Clair Drake and Horace Cayton, *Black Metropolis: A Study of Negro Life in a Northern City*, vols. I and II (New York: Harper, Row, 1945; 1962); see also Arnold R. Hirsch, *Making the Second Ghetto: Race and Housing in Chicago, 1940–1960* (Chicago: University of Chicago Press, 1998).

36 Sugrue, *The Origins of the Urban Crisis*.

37 Harvey L. Molotch, *Managed Integration: Dilemmas of Doing Good in the City* (Berkeley: University of California Press, 1972).

38 Douglas S. Massey and Nancy A. Denton, *American Apartheid: Segregation and the Making of the Underclass* (Cambridge, MA: Harvard University Press, 1993).

39 Alex Kotlowitz, *There Are No Children Here: The Story of Two Boys Growing up in the Other America* (New York: Anchor Books, 1992).

40 Sugrue, *The Origins of the Urban Crisis*; Arnold R. Hirsch, *Making the Second Ghetto: Race & Housing in Chicago, 1940–1960*. Chicago: University of Chicago Press, 1983; 1998).

41 William Julius Wilson, *The Truly Disadvantaged: The Black Underclass and the Making of Public Policy in America* (Chicago: University of Chicago Press, 1987); and William Julius Wilson, *When Work Disappears: The World of the New Urban Poor* (New York: Alfred A. Knopf, 1996).

42 Massey and Denton, *American Apartheid*.

43 Gregory D. Squires, *Capital and Communities in Black and White* (Albany: State University of New York Press, 1994).

44   Lincoln Quillian, "Migration Patterns and the Growth of High-Poverty Neighborhoods, 1970–1990," *American Journal of Sociology*, 105, 1 (July 1999): 1–37.

45   Louis Wirth, *The Ghetto* (Chicago: University of Chicago Press, 1928; 1956).

46   See, for example, Irving Howe and Kenneth Libo, *How We Lived: A Documentary History of Immigrant Jews in America, 1880–1930* (New York: New American Library, 1979); Nathan Glazer, *American Judaism*. 2nd edn. (Chicago: University of Chicago Press, 1972).

47   Beth S. Wenger, "Memory as Identity: the Invention of the Lower East Side," *American Jewish History* 85, 1 (March 1997): 3–27; Hasia R. Diner, Jeffrey Shandler, Beth S. Wenger, eds., *Remembering the Lower East Side* (Bloomington: Indiana University Press, 2000).

48   See, for example, Anthony M. Orum, *Introduction to Political Sociology*, 4th edn (Englewood Cliffs, NJ: Prentice-Hall, 2000) ch 8.

49   Robert Ezra Park, *Introduction to the Science of Sociology* (Chicago: University of Chicago Press, 1925).

50   John Higham, *Strangers in the Land: Patterns of American Nativism, 1860–1925* 2nd edn. (New Brunswick, NJ: Rutgers University Press, 1988).

51   See, for example, *2000 Statistical Yearbook of the Immigration and Naturalization Service* (Washington, D.C.: Immigration and Naturalization Services, 2000).

52   Roger Waldinger and Mehdi Bozorgmehr, eds., *Ethnic Los Angeles* (New York: Russell Sage, 1996).

53   Ivan Light and Edna Bonacich, *Immigrant Entrepreneurs: Koreans in Los Angeles, 1965–1982* (Berkeley: University of California Press, 1988).

54   Alejandro Portes and Alex Stepick, *City on the Edge: the Transformation of Miami* (Berkeley: University of California Press, 1993).

55   Roger Waldinger, *Still the Promised City? African-Americans and New Immigrants in Postindustrial New York* (Cambridge, MA: Harvard University Press, 1996).

56   See the excellent discussion of these matters in Linda McDowell, *Gender, Identity & Place: Understanding Feminist Geographies*, ch 2 (Minneapolis, MN: University of Minnesota Press, 1999).

57   Michel Foucault, *The History of Sexuality*, vol. I (London: Allen Lane, 1977).

58   Daphne Spain, *Gendered Spaces* (Chapel Hill, NC: University of North Carolina Press, 1992), pp. 15–16.

59   Daphne Spain, *How Women Saved the City* (Minneapolis, MN: University of Minnesota Press, 2001).

60   Manuel Castells, *The City and the Grassroots* (Berkeley, CA: University of California Press, 1983).

61   Wayne D. Myslik, "Renegotiating the Social/Sexual Identities of Places: Gay Communities as Safe Havens or Sites of Resistance?" ch. 10 (pp. 156–69) in Kristine B. Miranne and Alma H. Young, eds., *Gendering the City: Women, Boundaries, and Visions of Urban Life* (Lanham, MD: Rowman & Littlefield Publishers, Inc., 2000).

CHAPTER FOUR

Place Change and Continuity: The City in Global and Comparative Contexts

In 1626 Dutch official Peter Minuit "bought" Manhattan from resident Lenape Indians for the equivalent of $24. At that time, it was an Eden of fertile hills. Transformed by money and engineering, it became one of the most densely populated places on Earth – the crown jewel of capitalism![1]

The Dynamics and Resilience of Places

New York City, perhaps more than any other city, illustrates the dynamic and resilient nature of urban places. Its hustle and bustle as the financial capital of world capitalism and a huge ethnic cauldron has earned it "the city that never sleeps." The city and its residents have exhibited remarkable unity and strength after of the tragedy of a brutal terrorist attack on its economic core (the financial district) on September 11, 2001. Why and how do places possess this duality of dynamism and resilience? We began to address this central question in the previous chapter. **Capital** accumulation, social class, ethnic diversity and gender inequality, as we have shown from a historical perspective, not only have brought about drastic changes to urban places, especially in the United States, but have sustained some of their traditional patterns and characteristics such as entrenched residential racial segregation. Change and continuity of places, however, are no longer the products of historical forces within national boundaries. In this chapter, we focus on how global economic and cultural influences in more recent times have begun to transform local places on one hand, and sustain them on the other. Instead of just showing how urban places are being reshaped by globalization, we attempt to demonstrate that the new and old features of local places often result from both adaptation and resistance to globalization. In doing so, we examine sequentially the economic, political, cultural, and spatial dimensions of the global–local nexus and some of their interactions, avoiding giving analytical priority to any of these four dimensions. To the extent possible and appropriate, we will point to connections between the empirical examples and the theoretical perspectives discussed in chapter 3. Given the comparative thrust of this chapter, we place a greater emphasis on non-US cities, particularly by drawing from Chen's research on Chinese cities.

Pressure from above and Response from below: Economic Globalization and the Restructuring City

To begin with, urban places are grounded in and sustained by economic activities. Without a solid local economy of some kind, cities, large or small, tend to lose their source of existence. When the local economy experiences continued growth, a city generally prospers. When the local economy declines and then enters a sustained stagnation, a city can become lifeless. When the local economy rebounds from weak growth, a city can return to its former vitality. The fortune of places, however, is not always tied to the general cycles of economic upturns or downturns. Instead, it is tied closely with the particular type or mix of a city's economy and its capacity of responding to economic change. Moreover, the economic life of one particular city can be heavily influenced by its relative position and role in a system of many cities.

At the beginning and early stages of urbanization dating back centuries, the economic base of urban places was quite simple and undifferentiated. There was a relatively low degree of specialization in one single economic function, even though a few cities became heavily specialized as trading ports such as Genoa of Italy in early European urbanization. As a result of broader trade and industrialization, cities became more functionally differentiated places. While some cities, generally of larger sizes, developed more comprehensive and diversified local economies with different industries, others maintained their existing specialized functions even as they became more economically complex. For example, many of the historical trading ports continued to function as such after becoming major manufacturing centers such as Shanghai in China, Pusan of Korea and Kaohsiung on Taiwan. The economic structure of individual cities has shifted over time as they have become more integrated into a spatial system based on a territorial division of labor.[2] Think of this system as shaped in a pyramid. At the top layer of the pyramid stand a few large cities with more comprehensive and diverse functions. As we move down toward the broad base of the pyramid, we tend to find a larger number of smaller cities or towns that are functionally more specialized. The extent of a city's functional specialization is generally associated with its hierarchical location in the pyramid-like urban system. In contrast to this human ecological view, the critical perspective, generally of a political economy/world systems bent, would emphasize unequal power of and exchange among places in a system as a source of their relative positions and functions.[3]

In the lengthy history of urbanization, the economic bases of cities have changed frequently and continuously, while some functions of cities have remained largely stable. For a long, long time, most of economic change and continuity in urban places have stemmed largely from local sources and within local boundaries. When changes occurred from within, they tended to be relatively slow and gradual and of lesser magnitude due to the lack of strong stimuli from external source of influence. Local economic structure also tended to sustain itself when urban places were more closed to outside forces. Although there was long-distance trade among places for many centuries, its impact on local economic change was somewhat limited due to the small number of these trade ties and the small quantity and time-consuming nature of this trade. In addition, even when this trade spread beyond local places, it tended to be confined to regional and national markets as within-country functional and transportation ties among places improved. Most importantly, the bulk of the investment for producing goods for either local consumption or export originated from local sources. Even in the modern era of American industrialization in the eighteenth through the nineteenth century, locally based and family owned capitalists provided the dominant source of investment for factory production and jobs.[4] This tradition set the stage for the typical one-company town and some newly built factory towns in urbanizing America to rise and thrive in the late nineteenth and first part of the twentieth century. Local growth and prosperity during these times, however, had a lot to do with the emergent use of new machines and a captive labor market, which tied the increasingly skilled workers down to these communities.[5] Despite being interrupted by the Great Depression period, this local economic stability sustained amidst national growth and prosperity from World War II through the 1950s and into the entire 1960s.

The growing international influence on places

While international trade and investment had been around and affecting national economic performance for a long time, it began to exert a more visible effect on the regional and local levels from the early 1970s. The competition of imported consumer goods from low-cost producers like Japan and then Korea and Taiwan forced US manufacturing companies in older industrial cities to reduce costs by moving factories to suburban locations, to the newer cities in the American South and Southwest, and even to overseas sites. On the other side of the Pacific, rapid industrial expansion, which required spatial concentration of production assets and labor, fuelled the rise of large manufacturing centers in the newly industrializing economies in East Asia such as Hong Kong and Seoul.

This intensification of international competition and division of labor began to reorganize national and local economic spaces. This became a most striking phenomenon in the United States. With the movement of factories to the so-called "Sunbelt" and overseas, deindustrialization occurred and then accelerated in older manufacturing centers of the Northeast and Midwest. Horizontally, we saw a spatial redistribution of industrial capital, labor, and output across regions. In a hierarchical sense, the cities with declining manufacturing output lost functional influence relative to other cities of similar sizes in the urban pyramid. The real impact of this industrial and spatial restructuring, however, was felt at the local, community level, especially for traditional company towns. When capital moved away and factories relocated, the economic anchor of local places was largely lost. As a consequence, the social attachment to places also became eroded, although this erosion varied from place to place.[6] The disrupting economic and social impacts of accelerated capital mobility on local places became clear through David Harvey's theorizing on the transition from Fordism to flexible capital accumulation and Sharon Zukin's analysis of the contrast between market and place in the growth and decline of specific cities and parts of cities.[7]

Local places becoming increasingly globalized

The impact of the world economy on local places has become much more direct and intensive during the 1980s and 1990s and into the twenty-first century, which may be regarded as the era of real globalization. This impact originates from but is not limited to these trends:

- The growing importance of international trade and investment.
- The increasing global mobility of factors of production.
- The driving force of technology
- The growing importance of knowledge-based industries.
- The critical role of market size.[8]

While the spatial impact of economic globalization is uneven, cities, regardless of their size, location, and position in the urban hierarchy, have been affected and transformed in different ways. They have become increasingly denationalized and differentially linked to a globalizing economy.

New York, London, and Tokyo have become truly global financial centers that exert dominant power over the world economy and an emerging transnational urban hierarchy (also see chapter 2).[9] Other international centers like Miami, Toronto, and Sydney also have developed global city functions in banking, even though they might not become actual global cities, themselves.[10] The consolidation of the banking industry, facilitated by globalization, has led to the emergence of some second-tier national-level cities into new banking hubs such as Charlotte, North Carolina. Through mergers with two large rival banks locally and in San Francisco, Charlotte-based NationsBank became the second largest bank in the country in 1998. It pushed the city up to be among the top five banking centers in the US in terms of total deposits. The rapid expansion of the banking sector also fueled a boom in the construction of corporate complexes in Charlotte's central business district,[11] while this southern city has experienced some degree of hollowing out through suburbanization like the older northern industrial cities.

Another striking feature of this era of much stronger and direct global–local ties is that many more of the smallest of cities at the bottom of the national urban system are caught up in the global economic crosswinds. Lima, Ohio (population 48,000) lost a British Petroleum (BP) refinery in 1997 due to the company's global restructuring. This decision to close down the plant by BP's remote headquarters in London cost the small American city 500 jobs, a $31 million payroll, $26 million in annual fees to local utilities, and $11 million to local vendors. In addition to losing its economic lifeline, Lima was stripped of its very place identity because this was where John D. Rockefeller struck oil a century ago for Standard Oil Co., which merged with BP a decade ago; the city's flag bore an oil derrick.[12] In Shelby, North Carolina, a rural town, which used to depend on aged textile mills, Kemet Electronics Corp, a major local employer of newer and higher-technology products (compact disks, jet-aircraft components) since 1980, decided to dismiss 500 workers and move their jobs to Mexico in 1998. While many of these dismissed workers expected to find other jobs with other local or nearby companies in the booming Southeast region, they were concerned about the constant turmoil characterized by growth and retrenchment, hiring and firing, in today's cut-throat global economy.[13] These examples illustrate the delocalizing effect of economic globalization.

As the evidence on the US indicates, few cities or places today, regardless of size and location, are immune to the direct or indirect impact of economic globalization. Some cities have ridden the strong economic wind of globalization to consolidate or elevate their positions and functions in the urban hierarchy (e.g. New York, Charlotte). Other cities, especially some small manufacturing towns, and towns depending on a single industry mentioned above, have become very vulnerable to the competitive pressure of the global economy. There have emerged a variety of local places where specific

changes from the structural forces of globalization can be meaningfully studied and understood. Local changes brought about by global economic penetration, however, are not confined to an advanced industrialized country
like the US.

From local places to globalized spaces: evidence from China

As local places globalize, they are no longer local places in a traditional sense,
as has occurred in China over the past two decades. Chinese cities hid behind protective walls during much of the imperial times. While a number of
China's coastal cities were forced to open to Western commerce following
the Opium War during the second half of the nineteenth century, most of
the cities and towns remained largely closed to external economic influence.
This closure was heavily reinforced during Maoist China from 1949 to 1978
under central economic planning, after which vertical control was imposed
from above and self-sufficiency promoted at local level. The policy had the
cumulative effect of making Chinese cities insulated, cell-like localities with
hardly any horizontal ties and relatively little functional differentiation. The
rigid population policy through the institutional enforcement of the house-
hold registration system prevented rural to urban and inter-city migration.
This created a forced yet strong attachment to local places since residents
worked and lived in the same city or community for their entire lives. People
only moved under the special circumstances of organized population movements during the Cultural Revolution, when millions of urban youth were
sent to the countryside, or the government initiated job transfers between
cities. Ironically, the traditional local and inward orientation of Chinese cities and people's local attachment were largely maintained from imperial times
to and through the Communist era (see table 4.1).

   In the late 1970s and early 1980s, China began to reform its domestic
economy by weakening central planning and opening to foreign investment.
While urban reform didn't fully unfold until 1984, a large volume of direct
foreign investment, especially from Hong Kong, flowed into selected Chinese
coastal cities in response to their favorable locations and financial incentives.
When foreign investment began to generate rapid local economic growth in
these cities, they ceased to be Chinese cities of the past that depended exclusively on the administrative allocation of domestic capital. From the 1980s
into the 1990s, more Chinese cities were opened to foreign investment under the favorable and flexible policies that had previously been granted only
to the small number of coastal cities (see table 4.1).

   At the top of China's urban hierarchy, the most populous city of Shanghai
attracted the largest amount of foreign investment of any Chinese city during the 1990s, facilitated by aggressive central and local governments' policies of promoting the New Pudong Area. Realized foreign investment, a more

Table 4.1   A historical time line for recent Chinese history and urban development

Date	Key Historical Events	Urban Developments
1949	The Communist Revolution and the founding of the People's Republic of China.	Inheritance of a predominantly rural society, with a few large coastal cities such as Shanghai that experienced some Western influence.
1949–57	A shift from rural to urban-based industrialization; the government's first "Five-Year Plan" of 1953–57.	The emergence of a number of new industrial and mining cities; urban population grew from 27 million in 1949 to 54 million by 1957, with the proportion of the population in urban areas rising from 5.1% to 8.4%.
1957–61	The "Great Leap Forward" movement with heavy focus on heavy industries; the Great Famine occurred as a national disaster.	Continued urban growth: the number of cities rose from 176 in 1957 to 208 in 1961; the urban population grew to 69 million in 1961, making up 10.5% of the total population.
1962–5	The national adjustment period to rebalance light and heavy industries and to recover from the severe damage of the Great Famine to the agriculture.	Suppression of urban growth by mobilizing about 25 million city employees to return to the countryside; urban population declined from 69 to 67 million, with the proportion of urban population dropping to 9.2%.

Date	Key Historical Events	Urban Developments
1966–78	The Great Cultural Revolution caused severe interruptions to the national economy.	Urbanization was slowed further, with millions of urban youth being sent down to rural areas; urban population hovered between 60 and 70 million and the share of urban population averaged around 8.5%.
1979–83	The first phase of China's economic reform and opening, which focused on rural areas.	The creation of four special economic zones along the country's southeast coast for attracting overseas investment, especially from Hong Kong. The beginning of rapid growth and prosperity of selected coastal cities.
1984–8	The beginning of urban-based economic reform and wider opening to the outside world.	The designation of 14 coastal cities including Shanghai as "Open Cities" for foreign investment; accelerated urban growth, as the number of cities rose to 434 from 193 in 1978 and the urban population grew 20.7% per year and accounted for 25.8% of the total population in 1988.
1989–91	A period of retrenchment following the Tiananmen Incident in 1989.	Steady urban growth, as the number of cities rose to 479 by the end of 1991 and the proportion of the urban population increased slightly to 26.4%.

| 1992–2000 | The revival and deepening of economic reform focusing on restructuring state-owned enterprises. | Urbanization picked up pace: the number of cities jumped to 667 in 1999 (primarily through the redesignation of rural counties) and the urban population reached 389 million, accounting for 30.9% of the total population; increasing rural-urban migration, with the floating population reaching around 100 million. |
| The late 1990s | A shift of development focus to the interior (western) regions of China to redress spatial inequality. | By then, the economic and social disparities between coastal and inland cities had widened considerably.[15] |

reliable indicator of external economic influence than contracted capital, rose from just $3 million in 1981 to $364 million in 1988 and to $4.8 billion in 1999. The share of Shanghai's industrial output produced by foreign-invested enterprises jumped from 1.1 percent in 1990 to 55.4 percent in 1998.[14] The influx of foreign capital into Shanghai's banking and real estate sectors played a major role in an unprecedented construction boom, especially in Pudong, which totally transformed the landscape and skyline of the city.[15] These global economic influences have been welcomed and accepted as contributing to the policy objective of making Shanghai a Chinese global city that could compete with other global cities in high-tech manufacturing and financial services.

It may be fully expected that creating links with the global economy would revitalize a former major industrial center like Shanghai given its historical reputation, location advantage, and economic strength. The more dramatic impact of economic globalization on Chinese localities has manifested itself in the making and remaking of small and previously marginal places. No city exemplifies this process better than the Shenzhen Special Economic Zone. A fishing and farming town of 80,000 people in the late 1970s, Shenzhen exploded into a sprawling, modern industrial metropolis of over four million by 2000. The most powerful driver of this rapid growth was overseas investment, especially from nearby Hong Kong. Realized overseas investment skyrocketed from $15.4 million in 1979 to $2.8 billion in 1999.[16] It was estimated that 15 percent of the nearly $2 billion of infrastructure investment in Shenzhen during the period 1979–86 came from outside sources. During the entire 1980s, foreign investment accounted for an annual average of 26 percent of Shenzhen's total investment for capital construction and infrastructure development, trailing only slightly behind domestic bank loans (27 percent).[17] Not far from Shenzhen in China's Pearl River Delta was another story of miraculous city-(re)making with overseas investment. Formerly a rural township surrounded by rice fields, Dongguan has in little over 10 years became a huge industrial center that covers 2,520 square kilometers and has nearly five million people. In 1998 Dongguan became the third-ranked city of China in exports and foreign exchange earnings, behind only Shanghai and Shenzhen. This rapid growth was driven by over 3,000 Taiwan-owned enterprises, most of which are computer and electronics manufacturers, in Dongguan. The city has become China's largest producer of computer peripherals for the world market through the production and distribution network of Taiwanese companies.[18] This functional specialization has reinforced Dongguan as a local supply node of the globalized computer industry.

As highly localized Chinese cities under a closed national economy have been solidly incorporated into the global economy, the latter's impact can be said to be truly penetrating. For the first time in urban history, so many local places have become part of the global economic space, even though some of them are more deeply imbedded than are others. In the process, these local places have been variably transformed. While local places may have lost some capacity of resisting the pressure and change brought on by the global economy, they have to varying degrees managed to adapt to change based on their traditional orientation and strength.

CONTINUOUSLY LOCAL IN THE GLOBAL ECONOMY

While the threat of economic globalization to reorient and reshape localities is real, it is unlikely to wipe out local diversity and local autonomy. British geographers Amin and Thrift argue:

> One distinctive characteristic, as in the past, is the uneven distribution of tasks in the international division of labor to different locations offering specific attributes for capital accumulation. Another is the spatially differentiated assimilation and inflection of global imperatives, as the latter encounter places with distinctive, historically layered, socioeconomic structures and traditions. Globalization, therefore, does not imply a sameness between places, but a continuation of the significance of territorial diversity and difference.[19]

The persistence of economic localism can take varied forms. At the systemic or aggregate level, Persky and Wiewel found that an increasing share of economic activity in large US metropolitan areas continued to serve local markets, despite the expansion of traded producer services in global cities and other large metropolitan areas. Both local and internationally oriented activities grew at the expense of manufacturing production oriented to national markets.[20] Some individual small American cities have maintained past manufacturing bases and strengths through the local clustering of a particular activity, a geographically proximate network of manufacturers and suppliers, and dominating a niche market at the national rather than at the global scale. Illustrative US cities include Elkhart in northern Indiana, which has carved out a dominant position in manufacturing recreational vehicles (RVs) and Dalton in northern Georgia, which has sustained its reputation as the "carpet-making capital of America." A forced response to the ups and downs of the global economy came from the small northern Illinois town of Harvard (population about 8,000) located about an hour from Chicago. It has begun to find alternative development strategies since Motorola cut 80 percent of the 5,000 jobs in the local cellular phone manufacturing plant it had built in 1994. Ironically, the town was not pleased with the global electronics company's lack of involvement in the planned local revival, since John C. Galvin, the founder of Motorola, spend much of his life in Harvard and raised his sons there, who took over and moved the company to Chicago in 1928.[21]

Even as it is emerging as a Chinese "global city," Shanghai has maintained some of its distinctive local economic features. It continues to have a large, albeit slightly declining, manufacturing sector, as its service sector has grown rapidly in proportional terms (see table 4.2). Having lost much of its formerly dominant textile industry over the last decade due to competition, Shanghai has consolidated its other manufacturing strengths in automobiles, shipbuilding, and electronics, while also beginning to develop high-tech manufacturing such as chips and semiconductors in the Pudong New Area. While Shanghai's finance, insurance, and real estate (the FIRE cluster characteristic of a global city), grew in output relative to other service, the share of employment in FIRE in total service employment was only 2 percent in 1997, but did grow to 5.6 percent in 2001. The severe shortage of skilled professionals in FIRE indicates that Shanghai may be some ways off from becoming a world-class financial center. On the other hand, by sustaining and reconfiguring the old and new elements of its local economy, Shanghai has the potential to become a different type of global city rather than following the path and structure of New York or London.

In Taiwan, the Export Processing Zone (EPZ) at the harbor city of Kaohsiung, which was deeply integrated with the world economy as a low-cost production site and narrow export platform from the mid-1960s, has undergone an extensive industrial upgrading toward a science-and-technology park through automation since the 1990s. Despite the homogenizing

Table 4.2 Changes in Shanghai's economic structure and employment, 1978–2001 (selected years)

Indicator	Year					
	1978	1990	1995	1997	1999	2001
Agriculture's share of GDP (output)	4.0	4.3	2.5	2.1	2.0	1.7
Industry's share of GDP (output)	77.4	63.8	57.3	50.1	48.4	47.6
Services' share of GDP (output)	18.6	31.9	40.2	47.8	49.5	50.7
Agriculture's share of GDP (employment)	34.3	11.1	11.9	12.7	11.4	11.6
Industry's share of GDP (employment)	44.0	59.3	54.6	49.1	46.5	41.2
Services' share of GDP (employment)	21.6	29.6	33.5	38.2	42.1	47.2
GDP per capita (US dollar)	312	739	2,368	3,219	3,841	4,549

Indicator	GDP of the service sector by subsectors' shares					
	Year					
	1978	1990	1995	1997	1999	2001
Wholesale, retail, and catering	45.6	24.5	27.2	24.9	–	21.9
Transportation, storage, and communications	23.7	25.9	17.1	14.9	–	13.7
Finance and insurance	13.8	29.5	24.8	30.0	–	24.7
Real estate	0.5	1.6	9.2	9.6	–	12.6

Source: Various statistical publications and government documents on Shanghai.[22]

effect of economic globalization, it has unleashed new opportunities and spaces that allow various local places to refashion themselves in the light of specific traditions and shifting comparative advantages.

Local response to globalization via adaptation stems from different sources and domains. Industrial restructuring reflects an aggregate trend based on a collection of specific decisions of private enterprises to reposition themselves in global competition. Equally, if not more important, are a variety of policy responses from local governments to the pressure of economic globalization. Now we turn to looking at how a reorientation in local place politics and its policy-making process has begun to alter or reshape the fortune of urban places in the global economy.

Is Place Politics still Local? Relative Autonomy and the Restless Entrepreneurial City

As local–global economic links have become more direct and intensive (as shown above), there arises the crucial question of what forces now are capable of mediating this local–global nexus and governing local arenas where global economic processes unfold. The governing authority of nation-states appeared to have been weakened or reconfigured by strong global pressure and local responses, as a number of scholars have suggested,[23] and illustrated in figure 4.1.

The double-headed arrow denotes direct and strong global–local economic ties and interdependence, which we have examined in the previous section.

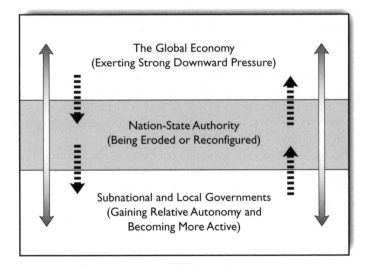

The Global Economy
(Exerting Strong Downward Pressure)

Nation-State Authority
(Being Eroded or Reconfigured)

Subnational and Local Governments
(Gaining Relative Autonomy and
Becoming More Active)

Figure 4.1   The squeezing of the state and the shifting locus of power.

As the dotted arrows suggest, the erosion or reconfiguration of state authority has occurred through losing regulatory or governing power to both the
supranational and local levels. From above global competition pushes states
to deregulate so that capital can move more freely, while states yield some
power regarding trade issues to such supranational entities as the EU and
WTO. From below subregional and local governments, especially the latter
have become more assertive in creating links with the global economy, thus
pressing national governments to shift more power to the local level. Due to
the constraints of limited revenues and bureaucratic drag, national states
have decentralized development decisions to subregional and local governments.

NATIONAL AND LOCAL POLITICS RESPONDING TO GLOBAL ECONOMICS

It is not a coincidence that the trend toward decentralized governance has
unfolded simultaneously with the acceleration of economic globalization over
the past two decades. In the United States, federal aid to states and municipalities has declined significantly under the Reagan and Bush Administra-
tions during the 1980s. This policy shift was brought about by the prevailing
neo-liberal ideology, which saw globalization as purely a market process and
any government intervention in support of people or places as leading to
suboptimal economic outcomes.[24] The considerably reduced funding by the
federal government began to put more pressure on local governments to seek
new and alternative sources of revenue to finance economic development.
This pressure has become particularly burdensome in a highly fragmented
urban governance system, which has long been characterized by regional
and local autonomy and financial independence. More and more state and
local governments have begun to aggressively pursue business opportunities offered by the global economy such as attracting direct foreign investment with financial incentives. The change in federal–state–local relations
regarding resource allocation has forced local places to interact more directly
with the global economy, which only reinforces the already strong global–
local economic nexus examined earlier.

   The ideology and rationale behind the nation-state's response to globalization through decentralization were not confined to the United States, and to
other capitalist industrialized countries such as Great Britain under Margaret
Thatcher, for that matter. They began to influence reforming state socialist
economies such as China and Hungary in the 1980s and state capitalist economies like Korea and Japan in the 1990s. In China, the adoption of an open-
door policy in 1980 pushed the state to reduce central control over the economy
and become more market conforming in policy making. This led to an important shift in decision-making power from the central to the provincial and lo-

cal government, which in turn created growing regional and local autonomy. While the Chinese system, characterized by much stronger central control and less local independence, differs considerably from the United States, it experienced the similar outcome of greater local autonomy resulting from less central support and greater devolution of central power.

Relative local autonomy in the US and Chinese contexts

Greater autonomy for local governments, however, is only *relative* given the constraints and changes in different national contexts. In the US context, urban governance is always decentralized and fragmented, with the state and local government holding and exercising considerable power through their differential taxing authorities over respective jurisdictions. State and local governments have gained further autonomy by way of less dependence on the federal government's resources. In the meantime, this enhanced autonomy is counterbalanced and circumscribed by the growing power of private corporations as a result of the federal government's deregulation policies in the 1980s. In this new environment, state and local governments not only are pressured to seek more available global business opportunities but have also become more vulnerable to the greater mobility and influence of global private capital that seeks local homes. We will illustrate the manifestations of this relative local autonomy in the US context below.

In the Chinese context, although the central government has ceded some power to provincial and municipal governments in recent years, it has maintained selected policy prerogatives and control mechanisms that set boundaries and parameters on how regional and local autonomy may be exercised. For example, the central government has scaled back some of the financial incentives such as tax abatements that were granted to the Special Economic Zone of Shenzhen earlier on. Nevertheless, by giving provincial and local governments the discretional power in approving foreign investment projects and setting prices and terms for land leases to overseas investors, the central government has allowed provincial and local governments to gain greater relative autonomy than in the US context. This similar trend toward decentralization and local autonomy in different national contexts has created opportunities for adopting varied economic development policies with different degrees of local economic success.

From a local sovereign to an entrepreneurial actor

In the face of a global economy, the local government in the United States has taken on a new orientation and role. Historically, according to Anthony Orum, the municipal government emerged as a public corporate body that exercised its sovereign powers in providing public services and regulations to meet the needs of a rapidly expanding local population and economy.[25] With the local economy becoming exposed to market competition at the global level, the municipal government has been pressed to give up some of its sovereign power and become an entrepreneurial actor in a new alliance with the state government and the private sector to pursue capital, jobs, and markets. The city government of Chicago, for example, has designed different incentives to eligible businesses to expand or relocate locally. The City can finance up to 100 percent of project costs for acquisition of fixed assets, renovation, and new construction for companies that create jobs. With the City's participation, banks can provide lower interest rate loans to eligible industrial and commercial businesses that are expanding/relocating within the City's limits. The City also administers the Tax Increment Financing (TIF) program, which offers financial incentives to developers and businesses to stimulate new development.[26]

While the above incentives may not be very new, the City of Chicago has started an aggressive initiative in recent years by working with World Business Chicago (WBC), which is a public–private economic development corporation co-chaired by Mayor Richard M. Daley and President of Aon Corporation. The mission of WBC is to expand the Chicago regional economy through the growth of the private sector. In joining this partnership, the City of Chicago has tried to reinvent itself as "continuously reviewing, updating, and streaming regulations and processes, committed to e-government, putting more forms and applications on-line, as well as introducing technologies to make government work faster and smarter."[27] Effort like this has paid off. In conjunction with aggressive marketing by WBC, Mayor Richard Daley, working together with Governor George Ryan, presented an incentive package worth $41 million over 20 years to the Boeing Company, which relocated its world headquarters from Seattle to Chicago over Denver and Dallas/Fort Worth in 2001.

From the private sector end, some local business leaders have begun to exert the influence of shadow government by lobbying local politicians to be more cosmopolitan in dealing with foreign companies. In Spartanburg and Greenville, South Carolina, a few corporate leaders helped the local governments shape an industrial foreign policy that has successfully attracted a heavy clustering of German automotive manufacturing facilities, which earned it the nickname "the autobahn." According to Rosabeth Kanter who studied this region as a case of local economic success, the presence of international companies created and spread the concepts, competence, and connections of world-class operations and thus stimulated improvements in local American companies. She suggested that these may be more important benefits from the global economy for the localities than the usual measures of capital infusion and job creation.[28]

Greater relative autonomy may foster local economic success but doesn't guarantee it. First of all, there is the question whether the overall long-term benefit from the infusion of capital and the construction of a new factory will outweigh the protracted cost of continued tax incentives. Secondly, there may be built-in limits to providing alluring incentives in the localized political system. Too much tax incentives could erode the local revenue base and thus burden the local property taxes, which may weaken funding for local schools. This could in turn lower the quality of education, which defeats the purpose of attracting capital and jobs with well-trained labor in the first place. Finally, increasing inter-local competition for capital and jobs with financial incentives cedes more bargaining power and leverage to more spatially mobile private corporations. Their tendency to seek the next lower-cost location will always make local governments vulnerable to the loss of recently gained economic benefits, thus pressuring them to use the relative autonomy to compete for the next round of opportunities.

From political control to market guidance

The local government in China has gained relative autonomy in a different political context. This shift was set in motion by decentralization in 1979 when China's central government designated only Guangdong and Fujian as provincial experiments for foreign trade and created four special economic zones on the coast of the two provinces as the first locations open to foreign investment. This location-specific policy was intended to target overseas Chinese investors with social, cultural, and geographical connections to that part of China. Provincial and local governments were given greater authority to approve investment projects and allowed to levy lower taxes on joint ventures. In the late 1980s, the central government adopted a set of policies that targeted Taiwanese capital through the creation of Taiwan Investment Zones in the coastal cities of Fuzhou and Xiamen facing Taiwan (see table 4.1, p. 102).

Local governments in Guangdong and Fujian Provinces have become market oriented at two levels. At the institutional level, they have become effective *generators* and willing *providers* of financial resources and policy incentives that reinforce the positive impact of primarily overseas Chinese capital on local economic growth. As a result of fiscal reforms, which defined localities' share of the tax revenues, local governments have got the right to keep the fiscal surplus. The more growth and revenues that could be generated, the more surplus revenues local governments could keep after turning in their share of the tax. Thus, local governments have become more motivated to make economic development the top priority. In the cities of Guangdong and Fujian, investing surplus revenues heavily in physical infrastructure has become a common strategy for generating more growth. In Shenzhen, which lacked physical infrastructure for being a newly created special economic zone, the local government poured massive investment of its surplus from earlier growth into the construction of roads, factories, and power and telecommunications facilities. This considerable upgrade of infrastructure has led to sustained economic growth and the rapid development of higher technology industries. In the city of Dongguan, both municipal and township governments are particularly willing to offer financial incentives such as reduced land prices, factory leases, and utilities charges to Taiwanese investors. The Taiwan Affairs Office of Dongguan provides special services to Taiwanese investors in processing entry and exit travel documents, clearing traded goods, settling economic disputes, maintaining public order, and arranging for child education. These favorable policies and practices have helped make Dongguan the most popular and concentrated locality in China for Taiwanese companies to set up factories, which account for roughly one-third of all Taiwan-invested factories in Guangdong Province.[29]

Irrespective of the different political contexts, the examples from both the United States and China illustrate a convergent new localism phenomenon, which involves city officials taking on a strategic broker role in attracting new businesses and upgrading their position in a global urban hierarchy.[30] This new local politics, however, is no longer local, but has evolved and adapted to become globally oriented and practiced.

Places with Hybrid Imprints: Global Consumerism and the Shifting Local Cultural Landscape

As a new brand of the local government has begun to reshape the fortune of places in response to economy globalization, the social and cultural appearance and meaning of places have been undergoing a metamorphosis. While general cultural change at the national level tends to be slower than and lag behind economic growth, the spread and penetration of global economic forces and global consumerism have accelerated cultural change at the local level. Instead of being shaped merely by global economic processes, urban culture in a global era takes on a dynamic and identity that reflect both the diffusion from and adaptation or resistance to an emergent global culture. Therefore, urban or place culture deserves a focused examination for improving our understanding of the new content and meaning of urban places. We focus primarily on the behavioral and spatial aspects of an emergent consumer culture in Shanghai in response to both Western commercial penetration and the inertia of traditions, while giving secondary attention to other physical and symbolic forms of the changing urban culture in both Chinese and US local contexts.

To facilitate this examination, we draw from the theoretical insights of a couple of scholars reviewed in chapter 2. The three elements of Henry Lefebrve's thinking – **spatial practices, representation of space**, and

representational spaces (see chapter 2 and the Glossary) – provide a general guidance for looking at both the material aspect and symbolic meaning of urban consumer culture. Sharon Zukin's work offers more relevant and specific arguments and analytical concepts that can help reveal the implications of our empirical examples. She argued that the spread of global cultures tends to make place more homogeneous in some ways and heterogeneous in others. To study the cultural reconfiguration of place, Zukin has applied the conceptual prism of **landscape**, which refers to "both physical surroundings and an ensemble of material and social practices and their symbolic representations."[31] In a later book, she argued more specifically that "the growth of cultural consumption (e.g., food, fashion, tourism) and the industries that cater to it fuels the city's symbolic economy and its visible ability to produce both symbols and space."[32] In addition, British sociologist Leslie Sklair suggests that the cultural–ideological project of global capitalism "is to persuade people to consume above their own perceived needs in order to perpetuate the accumulation of capital for private profit..."[33] While we are in general agreement with these observations, we should not assume a broad and ready local acceptance of the prevailing global consumerism, while neglecting varied local adaptive responses to it. We need a more nuanced argument in this regard to set up the empirical examples.

GLOBAL HALFWAY? CHANGE AND ADAPTATION IN LOCAL CONSUMER CULTURE

Prior to the broad spread of global consumerism over the last two decades, cities in most developing countries exhibited a fairly undifferentiated landscape that displayed physical and symbolic features of traditional national cultures with some varied regional and local flavors. This pattern was largely predictable in that it was a basic product of more or less closed national economies and isolated local economies. Even in a few large metropolitan centers, which might showcase some influence of the Western commercial culture, the latter remained institutionally and spatially confined and segmented relative to the dominance of local consumption. While the marginal position of Western commerce on the local cultural landscape could be partially attributed to state regulation, it also was associated with the lack of purchasing power and awareness on the part of local consumers. The cultural landscape in Chinese cities prior to 1980 was even more bland and monotonous than many Third World cities due to the government's promotion and organization of cities as production rather than consumption centers. Even in the once most cosmopolitan center of Shanghai, government guided spatial planning of many years left behind a "gray" urban landscape dominated by the heavy clustering of factories and low-rise apartment buildings, with little space for shopping centers and public recreational facilities. This landscape was also barren in that it was devoid of any physical symbols of commercial advertising such as billboards. The wide opening of traditional Chinese cities to Western consumerism has begun to create a new cultural landscape that is unfolding with visible local features.

Although cultural change must occur in a place penetrated by global economic and cultural forces, this change may not be unidirectional or linear leading to convergence toward the global norm given the constraint of local contexts. Therefore, the degree and scope of the impact of global consumerism on localities in any given period depend on the balance between the power and penetration of global forces and the strength and depth of local factors. While global consumerism infiltrates through such mechanisms as aggressive advertising and marketing to generate local demand, major countervailing local factors include the span of institutional regulation and the persistence of traditional values, customs, and ways of life. From the *cultural meaning perspective*, as opposed to the *global* or *imported perspective* in cross-cultural consumer research, individual consumers not only are attracted to a product's specific attributes, but also appreciate the culturally based meanings that are embodied in the product and consumption act.[34] Therefore, we argue that the emergent local cultural landscape may feature a hybrid imprint of global consumerism and local adaptation. The two not only co-exist but also reinforce each other to create both tension and complementarity in local places.

THE GLOBAL AND THE LOCAL IN SHIFTING CONSUMER CULTURES

While recognizing the co-existence and mutual reinforcement of globalization and localization, Rosenau predicts the eventual triumph of globalization over localization.[35] Others have suggested the structuring effect of the global on the local, which is contingent on the global.[36] This argument appears to receive strong support in the realm of consumer culture, given the powerful impact of global (primarily Western or American) consumerism on local places, especially those in developing countries. The evidence, however, points to different forms and degrees of local expressions and resistance.

We begin by showing the evidence on local areas in urban America where one would expect a well-established and saturated presence of US global corporations that are projecting their influence to overseas localities. An example from Chicago demonstrates otherwise. In many of the fast-changing areas going through renewed gentrification such as Wicker Park and Logan Square, Starbucks – an increasingly visible symbol of American globalizing corporate influence and cultural lifestyle[37] – has been expanding locally. It has even opened a store across the street from Cabrini-Green, which has been changing slowly from a former enclave of high-rise public housing projects to a more trendy neighborhood with newly constructed upscale condos and townhouses. To respond to the displacing effect from the intrusion of the new cultural symbol and wealth, local residents have staged protest in many forms including a documentary film called *Voices of Cabrini* and neighborhood organizations like The Coalition to Protect Public Housing. Likewise, the President of the Chamber of Commerce for the predominantly Mexican Pilsen community in Chicago, spoke out against global corporations moving into ethnic areas: "I don't think Starbucks could cut it in Pilsen. If they tried, we could ask questions. Who's their clientele going to be? What are their hiring practices? How would they make themselves fit in?"[38] Here we have witnessed the new local expansion of global corporations and local resistance to it that reflect a strong sentiment to preserve neighborhood integrity and ethnic diversity. This effort, however, is more difficult to organize and sustain in the face of the accelerated pace and spread of gentrification in many of the central city minority communities.

In Chinese cities in general and particularly in Shanghai and Beijing, the impact of Western (American) corporations and consumer culture has been greater while local response to it has featured acceptance, imitation/competition, and modification alternatively. In 1999, a basketball tournament run by Nike drew 1,600 Shanghai teens, many of whom lined up for a chance to shoot over a life-size cutout of American sports icon Michael Jordan who is "the most popular man in China who's never been to China."[39] When 1,000 Chinese respondents were surveyed to name the best known Americans, Michael Jordan finished second (just behind Thomas Edison by a narrow margin), and ahead of Albert Einstein, Mark Twain, and Bill Clinton.[40] Approximately 60 McDonald's restaurants in Shanghai (and 84 in Beijing alone) have made their way into traditional residential areas other than their prominent presence in and around downtown commercial districts. Since 1989, when the first Kentucky Fried Chicken restaurant appeared in Shanghai, cumulative sales had reached $300 million by 1999 and the number of KFC outlets has increased by 100 a year for the last two years, to about 600 nationally today. A consumer survey in Shanghai[41] showed that the hamburger ranked at the top of preferred fast foods (see figure 4.2 below).

The embracing of the American fast food in Chinese and Asian cities has broadened and deepened to such an extent that it has become almost locally internalized. In one recent survey, nearly half of all Chinese children under 12 identified McDonald's as a domestic brand. With over 2,000 restaurants in Japan, McDonald's Japan is the largest McDonald's franchise outside of the United States. The story is told of a little Japanese girl who arrives in Los Angeles, looks around, sees a few McDonald's, tugs her mother's sleeve and says to her "Look, Mom, they have McDonald's in this country."[42] While the large number of McDonald's restaurants may have blended into the local

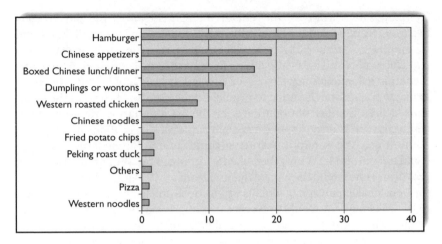

Figure 4.2   Types of fast foods preferred by consumers in Shanghai.

landscape and into the minds of young consumers, they remain a distinctive symbol of the power and appeal of American culture that stands apart from and yet connected to the local scene. Research has shown that younger and more affluent consumers in Beijing go to McDonald's to have a special experience of connecting to America and the outside world. Although he didn't quite like the taste of the Big Mac, one consumer likened the experience to sitting in a restaurant in New York or Paris, a sort of "instant emigration" or cheap trip to an alluring distant land. These McDonald's goers also regard the fast food outlet as a new social space where they can socialize and relax with friends, colleagues, and business associates. The experience allows them to feel more modern and part of a higher social status.[43] This empirical evidence in the Chinese context illustrates Sharon Zukin's general argument that culture can symbolize "who belongs" in specific places. It also, in a different way, lends credence to her specific point about restaurants being capable of indicating social distinctions and synthesizing global and local cultures.[44]

The second type of local responses to American fast food involves simultaneous imitation and competition, which complicates the consumer cultural landscape further. Variations of American fast food have cropped up in places of divergent national cultures. In Paris, a city known for its long tradition of fine cuisine and where a French farmer vandalized a McDonald's restaurant a few years ago and became a "national hero" for it, there is a large number of fast-food croissanteries. The war-ravaged Beirut of 1984 witnessed the opening of Juicy Burger, with a rainbow instead of golden arches, whose owners hoped to build the "McDonald's of the Arab World."[45] This imitation of both format and content took on a competitive side in Beijing and Shanghai in the late 1980s when more than a dozen different local fried chicken shops emerged to wage a "war of fried chickens" against the popular Kentucky Fried Chicken. A common localizing strategy was to emphasize special Chinese species and sacred recipes that supposedly add both nourishing and curative values to the dishes.[46] The Shanghai-based fried chicken chain – *Ronghua* Chicken (Glory China Chicken) – opened its first store directly opposite of the KFC restaurants in Beijing. With the combination of fried chicken with a special flavor, steamed rice, and simple meat or vegetables dishes ready to be served, Ronghua Chicken was trying to compete with the KFC at its own game in terms of convenience, simplicity, and relatively low price. But the local indigenous competitor lost out eventually, as consumers strongly preferred the new and standardized (consistent) taste of the KFC and its clean restaurants with a more modern decor and friendly service. The local success of Western fast food in China also is attributable to its functional advantage of time-saving convenience that appeals to the youthful population who live a much faster-paced life today. In Japanese cities, as more women are working rather than preparing meals at home, McDonald's restaurants offer a sensible alternative, which partly accounts for the fast food chain's phenomenal local expansion and presence.

While a particular Chinese fast food lost in face-to-face competition, the concept of copycating and franchising with a local orientation has caught on, for both economic and cultural reasons. Each new Western chain store seems to have generated a slightly cheaper domestic clone nearby, helping spread lifestyle changes to the masses. The Chinese-owned copycat stores tend to cater to Chinese who cannot quite afford the imports.[47] In Shanghai and Beijing, a number of old-brand-name, indigenous restaurants and shops, some of which go back a couple of hundred years, have opened up branches to meet the growing demand tinged with a nostalgia for the traditional dishes and special food items of unique and colorful Chinese names. Some of these branch restaurants are crowded with diners of all ages in any given evening. A recent Gallup poll conducted in China indicated that 80 percent of consumers favored local brand names, and that seven of the top ten brands ranked according to name recognition were Chinese. *Wahaha*, a Chinese soft drinks brand, outranked Coca-Cola.[48] The "invasion" of Western fast food and stores has ironically enlivened national and local Chinese brands, which enriches the consumer cultural landscape in such Chinese cities as Shanghai and Beijing.

Other than the outright acceptance and imitation of and competition with global consumer goods, which have created a mixed local scene, modified adoption because of strong traditional preferences has added greater diversity and complexity. For example, the American snack food of Cheeto's marketed in Chinese cities is seafood-flavored. While imported cheese and Italian-style tomato sauces have made inroads into traditional Chinese cooking, a small number of upmarket restaurants have begun to create fusion cuisine. It involves Western staples such as beefsteak covered with hoisin and mango sauces, or wok-fried fish with a creamy base.[49] In the McDonald's restaurants in Indian cities, the Barbie doll in a Happy Meal wears a traditional *Ghara choli* (an Indian outfit with a long skirt, a blouse and a shawl or *dupatta*) with block heels, anklets and straight black hair and brown eyes, with a *bindhi* (the red dot on the forehead).[50] Having gone bankrupt, the famous Japanese name department store of Yaohan in Shanghai transferred ownership to a local competitor – Shanghai No. 1 Department Store – which then changed Yaohan's orientation from luxury imported goods to affordable local goods.[51] Finally, Starbucks has been gaining popularity with more than two dozen stores in both Shanghai and Beijing. However, after getting the permission to operate within the Forbidden City in central Beijing, the Starbucks store has to make its front and interior decor look more blended in with the surrounding traditional Chinese architecture, with only a small Starbucks logo outside the entrance (see plate 4.1). In this particular place of ancient history, the consumption of latte – a Western coffee and a symbol of a new and modern lifestyle – in a traditional tea-drinking culture has to be somewhat less obtrusive in a fusion of the global and the local.

The hybrid landscape of consumer culture not only exhibits the clash and complementarity between the global and the local, but also reflects the underlying tension between a modern economic trend and traditional cultural prac-

Plate 4.1   Starbucks in the Forbidden City in Beijing.

tices. In Shanghai, consumer demand for new and more spacious housing has fuelled the rapid construction of new and often luxurious high-rise apartment buildings in some old, traditional neighborhoods in recent years. In the case of one such building, which overlooks one of Shanghai's three famous Buddhist temples (Yufo Temple) from a short distance, the units did not sell very well. The reason was believed to be that potential buyers were turned away by a superstition that living in this building would bring bad luck since it towers over the temple, a sacred place of worship (see plate 4.2).[52] During Xiangming Chen's visit in 2001 to this neighborhood dominated by old-style one- or two-story houses, the modern high-rise also looked a little out of place, especially in contrast with what appeared to be the recently renovated temple in its traditional architectural style and strikingly-colored walls. As the case illustrates, entrenched cultural values can challenge the functioning of a strong real estate market at the local level, revealing a contradiction between the new, material and old, symbolic aspects of the urban landscape.

The cultural reconstruction of local polaces

Given the pace and scale of the spread of global consumer culture, we tend to see its homogenizing tendency that could wipe out traditional characteristics and practices in consumption and other cultural activities at the local level. Instead we have observed a more complex interactive process leading

Plate 4.2   Buddhist Temple and a highrise condo building in Shanghai.

to a sociocultural reconstruction of the local cultural landscape. This reconstructed landscape features both global and modern influences and local and traditional responses. While major developing country cities continue to be arenas for aggressive Western advertising and marketing, they are not passive recipients of the imported material culture. Most importantly, the local cultural landscape is in a constant state of reconfiguration in adapting to global cultural flows and forces.

Places Coming Apart and Together: Globalization, Local Spatial Inequality, and Inter-city Connectivity

In the economic, political, and consumer cultural realms, we have shown and discussed the inherently uneven impact of globalization on local places thus far. In this section, we focus on the local spatial consequences of globalization as manifested in the simultaneous tendencies toward greater inequalities between spaces and yet stronger connectivity between them. Ironic as it may seem, this reflects how both the fragmenting and integrating effects of global forces impinge on relations between local places. Differential links to the global economy benefit some places at the expense of others. This process has become intensified further in conjunction with more competitive policy-making at the inter-local level, as we have demonstrated previously. On the other hand, global economic and cultural flows have created stronger and closer ties between local places, including many formerly isolated and marginalized localities. The co-existence of local and inter-local inequality and connectivity does not depend merely on extra-local factors, but on the interaction between local traditions and new circumstances. Again, we stress the path-dependent nature of local place change, i.e. its pace and direction is always constrained by the cumulative influence of initial and evolving conditions.

Serious spatial inequalities within and between local places had existed long before the onset of intensive globalization over the last two decades. In fact, we have demonstrated in chapter 3 that social and spatial inequalities in the United States are a cumulative and sustained outcome of both historical and contemporary forces such as slavery, discrimination, and deindustrialization. These inequalities would persist without the recent local impact of globalization. However, there are new forms of inequality in an advanced economy like the United States that could be attributed to processes of globalization. More importantly, there are emergent spatial inequalities in developing countries that would not have arisen otherwise in the absence of globalization. Our goal is to present convincing evidence on the direct and indirect relations between globalization and local spatial inequality in a comparative manner, with a continued main focus on China.

CRUCIAL LINKS BETWEEN GLOBALIZATION AND LOCAL SPATIAL INEQUALITY

Globalization can produce inequality both within and between local places through social and economic mechanisms operating at different levels. With capital becoming much more mobile and its scope of flow much broader and more transnational, more places have become actual or potential target points for investment in the form of a new or relocated corporate headquarters or a manufacturing facility, a new shopping complex, or a new residential development. When there are more available and often competing sites, capital movement to find the best location has become more selective. The process has contributed to a reorganization of local places in the regional and national urban hierarchies and to a shift of local places into their new positions in an emergent global hierarchy. Some previously small and economically peripheral places have risen to higher-order cities through their direct and indirect ties with globalization. Other cities, which were once prosperous manufacturing centers, have declined and are trying to rebound by pursuing an alternative opportunity with or without global connections. While local places may rise or fall somewhat unpredictably in the global economy, the only predictable outcome is growing disparities between them.

In addition to the broad inter-local spatial impact of globalization, specific intra-city inequality has occurred as a consequence of global economic processes operating at the local level. Ironically, it is in the so-called global cities, which sit at the top of the global urban hierarchy, that spatial inequality has become most visible and serious. Spatial inequality in these places originates from the economic and social restructuring associated with globalization. Saskia Sassen has offered a clear explanation for this complex relationship through an argument that goes like this. The heavy concentration of producer services jobs (especially finance) in such global cities as New York and London leads to a rapid growth of highly skilled and high-paying jobs in and around the *Central Business District* (CBD). This trend has created a strong demand and also dependency for more low-end, low-paying service jobs such as office cleaning and hotel and restaurant businesses. The income polarization translates into new intra-city sociospatial inequality based on the differential residential choices and purchasing power of the high- vs. low-income service workers.[53] From the same perspective, Marcuse and van Kempen have suggested that globalizing cities could exhibit a reconfigured and more differentiated residential mosaic that consists of locations for the old elite and the new gentry (high-income professionals), the traditional working-class areas, and the ghetto of exclusion for the very poor.[54] It remains important to see how local spatial inequalities manifest themselves in cities or places that have experienced rapid globalization in recent years.

As Sassen has argued, spatial inequality has grown to such an extent that it has become a defining feature of the new social geography in the three global cities of New York and London, and to a lesser degree, Tokyo.[55] Has the same phenomenon occurred in other major cities that do not have the same economic functions as a New York or London, but are nevertheless globalizing into significant international centers? In the huge Indian city of Calcutta, which has been attempting to become a dominant center for such industries as petrochemicals and pharmaceuticals for South Asia, spatial inequality from its colonial days has persisted. The difference, however, is that class has replaced race (or caste) as the primary basis for division, as the low-income population has occupied the farthest area from the central city. Rio de Janeiro, Brazil has exhibited a very similar pattern of spatial division between the rich and poor as it has become increasingly deindustrialized. The central city is mostly non-poor, about 80 percent white, and low in illiteracy, while the periphery is occupied mostly by the poor, non-whites, and the illiterate. The poor remaining in the central city are concentrated in the infamous *favelas* (shantytowns).[56] Even such European cities as Amsterdam and Barcelona, which historically had relatively low residential segregation, have begun to exhibit more residential differentiation along ethnic lines, as they have absorbed more immigrants. The distinctive living quarters of northern African immigrants (mostly from Morocco) in Barcelona generally have lower housing quality, more crowding, and less appealing buildings.[57] Against this broad trend toward intra-local spatial inequality in both developing and advanced countries, we take a closer look at a couple of cases in the United States and China.

With a rich tradition as a site for studying spatial differentiation dating back to the Chicago School of Sociology (see chapter 2), Chicago remains instructional for understanding how historically rooted local spatial inequality may have evolved in its rise as a global city like New York and Los Angeles.[58] According to a systematic study of the transition of Chicago neighborhoods as ecological categories,[59] the old pattern of neighborhood divisions changed considerably from 1970 to 1990. What was classified as the transitional working-class neighborhood was the most dominant type in 1970, when it accounted for 45 percent of all census tracts, but it declined to only 14 percent of all neighborhoods in 1990. The stable middle-class neighborhood also shrank, though not as sharply, from 41 percent of all neighborhoods in 1970 to 34 percent in 1990. In the opposite direction, the ghetto underclass type of neighborhoods rose rapidly from only 3 percent in 1970 to 23 percent in 1980 and 31 percent in 1990. Likewise, the gentrifying yuppie category expanded, mostly in the 1980s, from 11 percent of all neighborhoods in 1980 to 21 percent in 1990. It is clear that with the increase in the two ends of the spectrum and the decrease in the middle categories, inter-neighborhood inequality in Chicago became more striking. In terms of timing and trend, greater local spatial inequality in Chicago was similar to what has transpired in other global or globalizing cities.

The specific mechanisms and characteristics of this local spatial transformation are more illustrative. The rapid growth of business service jobs stimulated a mutually reinforcing boom in the development of commercial offices, residential units, entertainment facilities, and retailing complexes in the original downtown and beyond. The Chicago downtown office sector was so "hot" that the developers of the 17-story Union Tower on the western fringe of the Loop District built the project in 1998 on spec – where lenders make loans for buildings in which developers have no commitments from anchor tenants. While both lenders and developers assumed significant financial risks in doing so, they bet the tower would be the first speculative building after 1990 to tap the increasing demand for space.[60] The residential market in the CBD also has been booming as 13,500 new homes, most of which were high-end condos, have been developed since 1990. Additionally, 5,800 apartment units have been converted into condos, creating an apartment vacancy rate around zero percent and rising rents.[61] This provides some corroborating evidence that the expansion of yuppie neighborhoods continued beyond the 1980s and into the 1990s. To cater to a growing number of affluent downtown residents, stores and theaters that abandoned downtown for suburbs for a long time have made a strong comeback. In 1999, a new $500 million, five-block shopping/entertainment complex on Michigan Avenue just north of the Chicago River opened. It includes a Nordstrom, a Virgin Entertainment Megastore, and a DisneyQuest indoor theme park.

The redevelopment and dressing-up of the Chicago downtown, however, has run head-on into the preservation of its old charm that reflects a complex realignment of local political, economic, and cultural forces. The case involved is a row of historic buildings that form a clifflike wall along the western edge of Grant Park on Michigan Avenue, known collectively to architects as the "Michigan Avenue streetwall." Not just beautiful, the buildings have a rich history, as the old Blackstone Hotel has hosted American presidents including Harry Truman and Richard Nixon. Mayor Daley and the City Council have wanted to protect these buildings from being the target of real estate developers by designating them in a special 12-block-long landmark district. The critical response to this measure came unexpectedly from prominent local architects. They complained that city officials, perhaps in overreacting to some perceived ugly features of the new hyper-modern buildings on Michigan Avenue mentioned above, tried to rein in their creativity by freezing these buildings into the equivalent of museums.[62] The architects appeared to have sided with a market-oriented approach against the vision and practice of using landmark designation to ensure that new development won't disrupt the historic character, which contributes to economic vitality by drawing people to live and work there in the first place. If this is the case, it is consistent with Sharon Zukin's claim that architects are increasingly susceptible to and influenced by the constraint of local real estate market and built environment.[63]

The reemergence of affluence in downtown Chicago has spilled beyond the original CBD through high-income gentrification in poor, declining areas and middle-income ethnic communities. In what has become known as the South Loop, new condos have spread through an area that was mired in physical decay and poverty for decades. Gentrification has accelerated in Wicker Park, an area originally settled by Polish immigrants and later by those from Latin America, from the late 1980s into the 1990s. While an average two-bedroom apartment rented for around $250 in 1987, the price doubled to $500 in 1990 and jumped to almost $1,000 by the end of the decade.[64] This process reflects the downward mobility of some transitional working-class and traditional middle-class neighborhoods discussed earlier. The direct, individual impact has been felt by the original residents in these gentrifying communities, who now confront the bleak prospect of being displaced and having to move elsewhere and away from their social support networks and kinship ties to a place that was once home.

Spatial inequality in Shanghai: how is it different?

It was almost impossible to imagine merely 20 years ago that intra-local economic and spatial inequality would ever occur in large Chinese cities. They were long characterized by a low and largely egalitarian wage across occupations and jobs set by the state and the undifferentiated pattern of residential settlement and monotonous apartment buildings regulated by government controlled urban planning. The last two decades, however, have seen dramatic changes in the economic structure and physical landscape of large Chinese cities, of which Shanghai is perhaps the most illustrative example.

Despite a very strong manufacturing tradition, Shanghai has experienced a rapid growth of its service sector in trying to become the primary international business center for China. The growth of services was led by finance, insurance, and real estate (FIRE), which became priority industries, while the traditional services (wholesale, catering) declined. FIRE accounted for nearly 40 percent of the GDP of the service sector by 2001 (see table 4.2 p. 106). Service employment, however, remains more skewed toward traditional services. In 2001, while wholesale, retail, and catering employed 28.7 percent of the service work force, finance and insurance had only 3.1 percent and real estate 2.5 percent.[65] Although these are very low percentages compared with those of London, New York, and Hong Kong, they have contributed to a widening of wage differences. In 1990, the ratio between the highest quintile and lowest quintile was 2.47, while it rose to 4.25 in 1999. The highest quintile grew sevenfold against 4.3 fold for the lowest quintile during that period. In 1999, average wage in finance and insurance in both state and non-state enterprises ranked at the top of 17 employment categories. In non-state enterprises, especially foreign-owned banks and insurance companies, average wage was twice as high as the second highest average wage for health workers.[66]

This rising income polarization, especially the emergence of a growing stratum of high-income business professionals, has fueled an active residential market that has created increasingly differentiated land and housing prices within and across various parts of the city. In 1999, the price for the combined use of Grade 1 developed land (around the CBD by the Hunagpu River) was seven times higher than Grade 6 at the city's periphery. Grade 2 developed land for residential use (near the CBD) could cost five times as much as Grade 7 land at the far edges of the city.[67] Flats in the newly built high-rise buildings in Pudong by the Huangpu River would sell for approximately $1,200 per square meter compared with less than $300 in other sections of the city. The expensive new housing developments along certain streets, about a 15-minute walk from the CBD, have become popular among the wealthy buyers, because they are very close to some newly opened Western style restaurants and coffee shops and not far from work. Given the rising demand, developers of properties intended for overseas sales, whose demand never fully materialized, have begun to discount units and re-target them toward higher-end domestic buyers. At the same time, developers of properties for domestic sales have begun to build "super-deluxe" units aimed at the highest end of domestic market. The outcome is a convergence in the previously two-tiered property market.[68]

The rapid but spatially uneven growth of new, expensive residential highrises has been accompanied by the demolishing of the old, one- or two-story houses with a distinctive Shanghai style in narrow allies that date back to the 1850s and became the most popular type of residence in the 1930s. Unlike the market-driven high-income gentrification in US cities, the municipal government of Shanghai has orchestrated the neighborhood-level redevelopment or renewal. From 1995 to 2001, the total demolished floor area amounted to 24.1 million square meters (see plate 4.3), which involved 526,232 households and over 1.6 million residents, more than one-tenth of Shanghai's total population.[69]

The displacing effect of this large-scale redevelopments is a bit similar to that of the smaller-scale high-income gentrification in Chicago. Many of the residents who have lost their old homes live on fixed, retirement pensions

Plate 4.3   Half-demolished traditional houses in front of modern highrises.

and may not get full market compensation from the government or developers for their demolished houses, especially those located at or near valuable areas such as the CBD, major shopping centers, or famous tourist destinations. Even with full resettlement compensation, some residents may not be able to afford to buy into the designated new high-rises. More importantly, some are unwilling to move into a very different living environment and leave behind the neighborhood and house wherein they have had strong social ties and emotional identity.

INTER-LOCAL SPATIAL INEQUALITY: ANY GLOBAL LINKS?

While growing intra-local spatial inequality can be traced to economic and social processes underlying globalization in both the US and Chinese contexts, is there any linkage between the global economy and change in traditional inequality between local places? Again, this relationship, if it exists, is shaped partly by the historical past and path of inter-local inequality in different countries. Any globalization induced change in terms of increasing or decreasing inequality between localities would not be possible without the built-in constraint of national or regional urban systems. Our examination of this issue continues with examples from the United States, primarily the Chicago metropolitan region and China in terms of uneven spatial development.

Although globalization has facilitated the emergence of new pockets of wealth and poverty in major US cities, the long-standing gap between central cities and suburbs has remained striking. However, the literature on world or global cities did not shift its analytical focus on the central city to the metropolitan features and manifestations of the global influence until the mid-1990s. In fact, the sectoral restructuring in the global city of New York began to involve its suburban ring as early as the mid-1970s. The suburban share of metropolitan employment in business services grew from 42.7 percent in 1974 to 63.6 percent in 1996, while the percentage of the city dropped correspondingly.[70] The same trend also has unfolded in the Chicago metropolitan region in sectoral and spatial terms. The Chicago portion of the metropolitan finance, insurance, and real estate (FIRE) employment declined from 77.2 percent in 1975 to 60.9 percent in 1995. The combined share of four rapidly growing suburban centers (Schaumburg, Northbrook, Oak Brook, Naperville) of the regional total rose from 1.7 percent to 10 percent during the same 20-year period.[71] Some of the suburban gain at the central city's loss came from the multinational corporations and banks in the region relocating their back offices or R&D facilities in the suburbs. The strong global economic presence in the region also is reflected in the spatial clustering of the local offices and distribution and warehousing facilities of major international corporations near and around the Schaumburg area, which provides them with easy and quick access to O'Hare International Airport.

The prosperity of some Chicago suburbs, or what Joel Garreau called "edge cities,"[72] has been accompanied by the decline of other suburbs in the region. A study commissioned by the McArthur Foundation in 1996 found a rapid dividing of the region's 262 suburban municipalities into camps of "haves" (rich suburbs) and "have nots" (poor suburbs). The former had grown with upscale housing and clean, taxable corporate offices, while the latter struggled hard with factory closings and social problems.[73] More recent evidence further confirms this trend. For a long time, Elgin, Aurora, Joliet, and Waukegan had strong local economies and vibrant identities as centers of manufacturing industries such as steel and machinery. They became called satellite cities, distinct from newer, more traditional (bedroom) suburbs that began to grow around Chicago at that time. With the decline and even disappearance of manufacturing in recent times, these localities have shifted to one-industry towns of a different kind – built around casinos and a tenuous new image. In Aurora, for example, Hollywood Casino is the city's second largest employer with 1,600 workers. In the meantime, the nearby suburbs (Gurnee, St. Charles, Naperville, Plainfield), while still trailing behind in population size, have surpassed the four old satellite cities in such critical indicators as median family income, spending and performance of local school districts, and violent crime rate.[74]

Decline has not been confined to these suburban cities away from Chicago.

A broader regional spatial restructuring also has encompassed the steady deterioration of some inner-ring suburbs such as Cicero, Harvey, and Hillside, which have become victims of both the departure of their residents and the spillover social problems from Chicago such as crime. It appears that several simultaneous trends have become overlapped and converged to create a new regional landscape of inter-local inequality. The renewed prosperity of the CBD has stretched its boundary outward unevenly. Residential decline and social ills that once affected some outer parts of the city have spread into the inner-ring suburbs. While a small number of suburbs have benefited greatly from the outflow of business service jobs from the city, other formerly industrial suburbs have lost out as they have lost most or all of their manufacturing jobs. Some of these trends and outcomes are directly related to global economic change and competition such as the downtown boom and the rapid decline of suburban-based manufacturing. The local impact of globalization on the decline of the inner-ring suburbs may be indirect through the demographic and residential transition of some communities around the city–suburban boundaries. Regardless of the causal conditions being direct or proximate, the cumulative outcome is an increasingly complex pattern of interdependent intra- and inter-local inequality as illustrated by the Chicago experience.

Inter-city inequality in China: both domestic and global sources

Just as at the intra-local level, inter-local inequality in China remained highly limited until the late 1970s under a highly centralized and redistributive system. To promote even regional development, the central government diverted resources from such better-off coastal cities as Shanghai to support the more backward interior cities. The vertical planning through administrative fiat, coupled with a promotion of balanced, almost de facto self-sufficient local economies, created and sustained cities and towns that were little differentiated in terms of industrial structure, housing standard, wage scale, and quality of life. This spatial pattern began to change in the early 1980s and has since been largely reshaped into a much more differentiated landscape by both domestic and global conditions.

Around 1980, the central government granted a set of favorable policies (e.g. special administrative status, tax incentives, targeted infrastructure investment) to specific coastal cities, thus privileging their development. These policies had a strong early impact on cities like Shenzhen and Guangzhou in China's southeastern region, which grew much more rapidly than most other cities. Around 1990, the favorable policies had been extended to Shanghai and other central and northern coastal cities, which formed the second wave and cluster of accelerated growth. By the end of the decade, with the cumulative effect of favorable policies and growth momentum, the cities along the entire eastern seaboard surged so far ahead most inland cities (see table 4.1 p. 103). By then, although the central government had already begun to extend favorable policies and to channel investment to the interior, especially the western region, inter-city and inter-region disparities had grown to a large degree. Accelerating this process was the increasingly stronger impact of direct foreign investment that flew disproportionally into the coastal cities in response to the earlier favorable policies and a better existing infrastructure. The domestic and global forces reinforced each other in producing a new spatial structure characterized by substantial inter-local economic and social disparities.[75]

Three indicators illustrate these gaps. First, in 1999, the top 10 cities, all in the coastal region, had a minimum of $1 billion in realized foreign investment. In contrast, realized foreign investment in the 100th–110th cities ranged between $53 and $43 million, while the bottom 10 cities on the list of 236 cites, all in the northwestern region, had zero. Secondly, the average annual wage of the top 10 cities was three times that of the bottom 10 cities. However, this indicator is deceiving given the continued state regulation of wages in various public agencies and enterprises that made up the city-wide average wage. In light of a much more revealing indicator, savings per capita for the top 10 cities were 10 times higher than that of the bottom 10 cities. Thirdly, the top 10 cities had a government expenditure per capita that ranged 10–20 times higher than the average of the bottom 10 cities.[76] This indicator, more than the first two, reflects the huge disparity in the aggregate wealth of the more developed vs. the less developed Chinese cities.

Due to the lack of metropolitan development, spatial inequality in China has grown more visibly between cities rather than between cities and their hinterlands. In fact, the differences and boundary between the urban core and the rural periphery in and around the more developed and prosperous regions (e.g. the Pearl River Delta) appear to have diminished or become blurred.[77] Inter-local inequality, however, is likely to continue growing on its own momentum, in spite of the state's policy to rebalance regional development. While this spatial outcome was not intended by the initial state's policy of favoring a few coastal cities, it has emerged predictably from the subsequent operation of local market forces and the impact of the global economy through direct foreign investment.

LOCAL–GLOBAL CONNECTIVITY: WHAT ARE THE SPATIAL CONSEQUENCES?

Triggered by global economic processes, spatial inequality at different geographical scales has a tendency to fragment places from within and outside. Greater connectivity, physical and otherwise, in the global economy is capable of integrating local places into networked spaces, with desirable consequences. These are not mutually contradictory trends, but are inherently linked and even functionally interdependent. Stronger and more direct ties to the global economy can foster the upward movement of some cities in the national or global hierarchy, thus creating new inter-city gaps intra-nationally and transnationally. On the other hand, these global–local ties might help to overcome barriers that tend to engender or maintain spatial inequality.

As we have discussed earlier in this chapter, an increasing number of cities, large or small, have become partially globalized local places. Here we suggest further that local places should be viewed as nodes in multi-layered networks that collectively constitute the global economic and urban hierarchy.[78] Moreover, we emphasize the importance of studying the different types of network ties among places as a useful way of understanding their functional characteristics and spatial outcomes. We illustrate how this may be done with examples of various types and scales of inter-place ties.

At the systematic level of inter-city ties, the network analysis by David Smith and Michael Timberlake has shown the shifting positions of international cities in a hierarchical world system by examining the frequency and volume of inter-city air passenger flows. Their recent study has revealed that a growing number of Asian cities (e.g. Seoul, Bangkok) have become more active and "central" in the world system of cities over the last 20 years as airline passenger flows through them have steadily increased relative to other cities.[79] This finding has alerted us to how a cluster or set of cities can rise or slide along a crucial functional dimension – air travel – which may have been strongly facilitated by their rapid economic growth. It is logical to expect that stronger and more extensive air travel connectivity among these cities will further their growth and other important functions in the world hierarchy.

In a more connected world system, an individual city may develop new ties to other cities on top of its existing strong linkages, thus solidifying or moving its position upward in the global hierarchy. In recent years, Chicago's Board of Trade and Mercantile Exchange, the largest exchanges of its kind in the world, have established trade links with the future and options markets in London, Paris, Taipei, and Buenos Aires. The Network Access Point (NAP), located in Chicago's Loop and operated by Ameritech Corp., has grown so fast that it may have become the world's busiest Internet connection point, an information technology equivalent of O'Hare International Airport.[80] While adding these new technology based external links, Chicago has maintained its traditional position as the nation's rail hub, even though it is the headquarters of just one major railroad. With the historical advantages in several thousand miles of track and 22 major yards, the system also has benefited from upgraded yards, computerization, standardization of locomotives, and cooperation between railroads.[81] The combination of the old and new ties helps sustain the competitive advantages of Chicago relative to other major international cities with strong transportation facilities.

CROSS-BORDER INTER-LOCAL TIES IN GEOGRAPHICAL PROXIMITY: THE ASIA-PACIFIC TRANSBORDER SUBREGION

Ties created through modern telecommunications and transportation technologies can overcome the barrier created by physical distance. This has prompted some scholars to go as far as to proclaim the end of geography.[82] Although the emergence of electronic space in global finance renders distance much less relevant, geographical proximity remains a salient factor in the development of inter-local ties in some intra- and transnational regional contexts. In the Asia-Pacific transborder subregions that Xiangming Chen has studied, geographical contiguity and proximity are a key to creating effective ties between border cities on different sides of the international boundaries. Many of these border cities, which have been neglected by their respective national governments for a long time, lack a well-developed transportation infrastructure, especially roads and railroads. Geographical proximity between international border cities ameliorate the barrier effect of borders, as it facilitates access to certain raw materials for convenient manufacturing and to river ports or seaports for shipping and export. Obviously, geographical proximity only has this desirable effect on inter-city ties across borders under the favorable conditions of more open borders and decent cross-border transportation infrastructures.

The Greater Tumen Subregion (GTS) in Northeast Asia is a case in point (see map 4.1). Consisting of the Yianbian Ethnic Korean region of China's Jilin Province, the northern border of North Korea, and parts of the Russian Far East (RFE), the GTS has been improving transportation ties near and across the borders, which were few and bad for a long time. Several main roads and railroads leading up to, along, and across the borders in the GTS have been completed. A highway between the Chinese cities of Hunchun and the Shatuozi crossing has been completed. A cross-border road now links the Chinese city of Yanji and North Korea's Chongjin port through the crossing at Sanhe on China's side. Another road originates from Yanji and goes through China's Shatuozi crossing to the Rajin port. A third cross-border road goes from the city of Tumen to Sonbong through the North Korean border town of Nanyang. A cross-border road for truck transportation may also be built from Hunchun through the Russian border town of Kraskino to

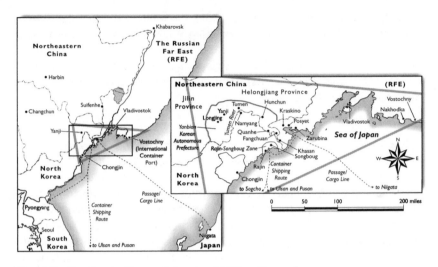

Map 4.1   The Greater Tumen Subregion (GTS) and beyond.

the RFE port of Zarubino. These inter-city transportation ties over borders, in conjunction with other conducive economic, political, and sociocultural factors (growing border trade, revived cross-border ethnic ties), have created better and more beneficial connections among previously isolated border cities and between them and the outside world. This has led some of the border cites, especially such Chinese border cities as Hunchun, which were severely underdeveloped due to their peripheral positions and lack of state support, to grow into important industrial centers with direct manufacturing ties to the global economy.[83]

Whether it is inter-city ties in air travel or financial transactions in a global hierarchy or inter-city ties that bridge long-closed border areas at a transnational subregional level, they carry important relational and functional consequences. Stronger ties allow some cities to rise at the possible expense of other cities' fall. In the Asia-Pacific transborder subregional context, however, it appears that improved cross-border transportation ties, reinforced by geographical proximity, may help lift more marginal places with shared prosperity, assuming there are other favorable factors at work also. The difference lies in how new external ties interact with the indigenous past of any local place as it adapts to the dynamic global system.

Forever In-between: Global and Local Forces in the Transformation of Places

In this chapter, we have examined the economic, political, cultural, and spatial dimensions of the increasingly close links between global processes and local places. These analytical dimensions are by no means independent of one another; instead they interact in multiple ways that lead to significant consequences at the place and individual levels. In responding to global economic competition, local governments in both advanced market economies and formerly centralized planned economies have taken on the vision and behavior of a more private sector oriented actor. Their switch to efficiency based policy-making can easily reshape the future fortune of places. The penetration of global or Western consumerism has altered the institutional, individual, and spatial aspects of the local cultural landscape in Shanghai. However, as we have shown, the local response has a mixture of flexible adaptation, outright imitation, and competitive resistance, which tends to yield a more hybrid consumer culture. In addition, while economic globalization has created intra- and inter-local spatial inequality directly or indirectly, this inequality may take varied forms depending on the local and national contexts. By examining each of the four dimensions separately and how they may relate, we hope to have conveyed a clear message that the global-local nexus is multifaceted and very complex.

If places are fundamentally important to the material and emotional well-being of their residents, as our central argument goes, then this chapter has enriched the thesis by showing how extra-local forces at the global scale can have a strong impact on local places to the extent of transforming them. In this sense, we have complicated further the nature, meaning, and functions of places. They matter a great deal more to people's lives than in the past because they are now exposed more than ever to forces beyond local boundaries. As places change as a result of varied global processes, they tend to lose the power of traditional institutions and practices that have sustained people's attachment to the places. Although we suggest that globalization has become a more important source of local change than domestic ones, we have demonstrated that global forces cannot resist becoming localized, at least partially, as the resilience of certain local traditions and practices create adaptation or even resistance to the external impact. Beyond these competing and perhaps complementary views on how modernity vs. tradition and the global vs. the local shapes places, we also may need to think of the changing meaning and nature of places in light of some postmodern dynamics discussed by David Harvey such as fragmentation, discontinuity, and chaos.[84]

Based on the argument and evidence in this chapter, we want to put forth a proposition: as globalization affects local places more directly and on more fronts, it is more likely to lead to interconnected changes. That is, the globalization of local economies tends to produce change in cultural traditions and practices with a shorter lag than previously. If different global forces have weakened traditional and somewhat separate spheres of local life, distinctive local institutions and activities are less likely to survive. Therefore, place change or transformation may become more common and enduring than continuities.

Finally, we can derive a practical lesson from clarifying the complex relationship between the global environment and the local place that may encourage a more promising future for the well-being of places. Even though globalization induces more intensive inter-local competition and thus contributes to greater spatial inequality, it creates stronger connectivity and interdependence among places that may foster cooperation. We echo those who have advocated a more cooperative relationship among local governments in the spirit and practice of new regionalism to bridge inter-place disparities within metropolitan regions (see chapter 5). At the transnational level, we see in the Asia-Pacific transborder subregions cooperative tendencies that constitute a bottom-up collective response to the unyielding impact of globalization from above. This phenomenon may also reflect the emergent reality of transnational urbanism grounded in diverse socioeconomic opportunities, political structures, and cultural practices of connected local places and actors within them.[85] Thanks to more efficient transportation and telecommunication ties accompanying globalization, we have become more aware of the importance of places closer to home or far away. Our future will depend more than ever on how we think and act to preserve that importance both locally and globally.

Notes

1   Joel L. Swerdlow, "Tale of Three Cities: Alexander, Cordoba, and New York," *National Geographic*, 196, 2 (August 1999): p. 53.

2   W. Parker Frisbie and John D. Kasarda, "Spatial Processes," pp. 629–66 in Neil J. Smelser, ed., *Handbook of Sociology* (Beverley Hills, CA: Sage Publications, 1988), p. 643.

3   See David A. Smith and Michael Timberlake, "Conceptualizing and Mapping the Structure of the World System's City System," *Urban Studies*, 32, 2 (1995), pp. 288–9.

4   See Anthony M. Orum, *City-Building in America* (Boulder, CO: Westview Press, 1995), chs. 3 and 4.

5   Sharon Zukin, *Landscapes of Power: From Detroit to Disney World* (Berkeley, CA: University of California Press, 1991), p. 7.

6   See Rhoda H. Halperin, *Practicing Community: Class Culture and Power in an Urban Neighborhood* (Austin, TX: University of Texas Press, 1998); Kathleen Stewart, *A Space on the Side of the Road: Cultural Poetics in an "Other" America*

(Princeton, NJ: Princeton University Press, 1996).

7   See David Harvey, *The Condition of Postmodernity: An Enquiry into the Origin of Cultural Change* (Oxford: Basil Blackwell, 1990), ch. 9; Zukin, *Landscapes of Power*, ch. 1.

8   Dennis A. Rondinelli, James H. Johnson, Jr., and John D. Kasarda," The Changing Forces of Urban Economic Development: Globalization and City Competitiveness in the 21st century," *Cityscape*, 3, 3 (1998): p. 73.

9   Saskia Sassen, *The Global City: New York, London, Tokyo*. 2nd edn. (Princeton, NJ: Princeton University Press, 2001), esp. chs. 5, 6, and 7.

10   Saskia Sassen, *Cities in a World Economy*, 2nd Edn. (Thousand Oaks, CA: Pine Forge Press, 2000), esp. chs. 5.

11   Ann Carrns, "In Charlotte, the Sky Really is the Limit," *The Wall Street Journal*, October 7, 1998, p. B14.

12   Paulette Thomas, "A Town Is Buffeted by Global Crosswinds," *The Wall Street Journal*, March 20, 1997, p. B1.

13   Michael M. Phillips, "Globalization Comes to a Southern Town," *The Wall Street Journal*, February 12, 1998, p. A2.

14   Shanghai Statistical Bureau, *Shanghai Statistical Yearbook 1998* (Beijing: China Statistics Press, 1998), p. 119; Jizuo Yin, chief editor, *A Report of Economic Development in Shanghai 2000* (in Chinese) (Shanghai: Shanghai Academy of Social Sciences Press, 2000, p. 299.

15   See Fulong Wu, "The Global and Local Dimensions of Place-Making: Remaking Shanghai as a World City," *Urban Studies*, 38, 8 (1998): 1357–77.

16   Shenzhen Statistics and Information Bureau, *Shenzhen Statistical Handbook 2000*, Shenzhen, China, 2000, p. 94.

17   Xiangming Chen, "The Changing Role of Shenzhen in China's National and Regional Development in the 1980s," pp. 252–79 in George T. Yu, editor, *China in Transition: Economic, Political and Social Developments* (Lanham, MD: University Press of America, 1993), p. 2.

18   Xiangming Chen, "Both Glue and Lubricant: Transnational Ethnic Social Capital as a Source of Asia-Pacific Subregionalism," *Policy Sciences*, 33 (2000): 269–87.

19   Ash Amin and Nigel Thrift, "Living in the Global," pp. 1–22 in Ash Amin and Nigel Thrift, eds., *Globalization, Institutions, and Regional Development* (Oxford: Oxford University Press, 1994), p. 6.

20   Joseph Persky and Wim Wiewel, "The Growing Localness of the Global City," *Economic Geography*, 70 (1994): 129–43.

21   Another irony of this place story is that a third son of John Galvin, Raymond "Burley" Galvin, remained in Harvard his entire life. He worked at the Harvard State Bank for 62 years almost up to the day he died at the age of 83 in 1980. Local residents saw him as an institution here, while his more famous relatives were jetting around the world to extend the global reach of Motorola. At a celebration marking his 50th year at the bank, he told a local newspaper reporter that "It was the joy of working with people and living in a small town and knowing everybody" that kept him in Harvard. See Mike Conklin, "Tuning out Motorola," *Chicago Tribune*, Tempo Section, February 21, 2002, pp. 1, 4.

22   *Shanghai Statistical Yearbook 1998*; *Shanghai Statistical Yearbook 2002* (Beijing:

China Statistics Press, 2002). p. 24; *A Report of Economic Development in Shanghai 2000* Jizuo Yin, chief editor. *Institutional Reform and Social Transition* (in Chinese) (Shanghai: Shanghai Academy of Social Sciences Press, 2001).

23 See James N. Rosenau, *Along the Domestic-Foreign Frontier: Exploring Governance in a Turbulent World* (Cambridge, MA: Cambridge University Press, 1997); Saskia Sassen, *Losing Control? Sovereignty in an Age of Globalization* (New York: Columbia University Press, 1996); Susan Strange, "The Erosion of the State," *Current History*, November (1997): 365–9.

24 See Susan E. Clarke and Gary L. Gaile,*The Work of Cities* (Minneapolis, MN: The University of Minnesota Press, 1998), p. 2.

25 See Anthony M. Orum, *City-Building*, ch. 2, pp. 17–18.

26 The Website of World Business Chicago (WBC), http://www.worldbusinesschicago.org/incentives.

27 Ibid. http://www.worldbusinesschicago.org/getting started.

28 Rosabeth Moss Kanter, *World Class: Thriving Locally in the Global Economy* (New York: Touchstone, 1997), pp. 242–3.

29 Chen,"Both Glue and Lubricant."

30 Susan E. Clarke and Gary L. Gaile, "Local Politics in a Global Era: Thinking Locally, Acting Globally," *The Annals of the American Academy of Political and Social Science*, 551 (1997): 28–43.

31 Zukin, *Landscapes of Power*, ch. 1, pp. 12, 16.

32 Sharon Zukin, *The Cultures of Cities* (Oxford: Blackwell Publishers, 1995), p. 2.

33 See Lesile Sklair, *Sociology of the Global System*, 2nd Edn. (Baltimore, MD: The Johns Hopkins University Press, 1995), chs, 2 and 3.

34 Hellmut Schütte with Deanna Ciarlante, *Consumer Behavior in Asia* (Washington Square, NY: New York University Press, 1998), p. 5.

35 Rosenau, "The Complexities and Contradictions of Globalization," *Current History*, November (1997): pp. 360–4.

36 Amin and Thrift, "Living in the Global".

37 Starbucks has expanded from fewer than 700 outlets in 1995 to 5,200 worldwide now. With its logo popping up across the world from China to the Gulf states, it has joined McDonald's as a favorite target of anti-globalization protestors. It has been accused of driving out independent cafes. See Alison Maitland, "Bitter Taste of Starbucks' Success," *Financial Times*, March 10, 2002; taken from *Financial Times* online at http://news.ft.com/ft/gx.cgi/ftc?pagename=View&c=Article&cid=FT3HQZ55NY Clive=true.

38 We thank Rachel Martin, an undergraduate student at UIC, who kindly allowed us to reference part of her final report for a Freshmen Seminar on globalization she took with Xiangming Chen in the Fall Semester of 2001.

39 Joel L. Swerdlow, "Global Culture." *National Geographic*, 196, 2 August (1999): 19.

40 Walter LaFeber, *Michael Jordan and the New Global Capitalism* (New York: W.W. Norton & Company, 1999), p. 135.

41 Xue Ling, "Digitized Fast Food," (in Chinese) *Branded Bulletin* (1999), p. 29.

42 Thomas L. Friedman, *The Lexus and the Olive Tree* (New York: Anchor Books, 2000), p. 296.

43 See Deborah S. Davis, ed., *The Consumer Revolution in Urban China* (Berkeley,

CA: University of California Press, 2000), chs. 6 and 9.

44 Sharon Zukin, *The Culture of Cities*, chs. 1 and 5.

45 George Ritzer, *The McDonaldization of Society: An Investigation into the Changing Character of Contemporary Social Life*, 2nd Edn. (Thousand Oaks, CA: Pine Forge Press, 1996), p. 2.

46 Yunxiang Yan, "Of Hamburgers and Social Space: Consuming McDonald's in Beijing," pp. 201–25 in Deborah S. David, ed., *The Consumer Revolution in Urban China* (Berkeley, CA: University of California Press, 2000).

47 For example, in Beijing the domestic Jing Kelong shopping warehouse opened next door to PriceSmart, a US chain, that opened its first store here in 1997 and plans to have 70 stores by the end of 2003. Aptly named, "Jing" comes from Beijing and the "kelong" is pronounced the same as the Chinese word for clone. See Elisabeth Rosenthal, "Buicks, Starbucks and Fried Chicken, Still China?" *The New York Times*, February 25, 2002; taken from *The New York Times* online at http://www.nytimes.com/2002/02/25/international/asia/25CHIN.html ?ex=1015657748&ei=.

48 Schlevogt, Kai-Alexander, "The Branding Revolution in China," *The China Business Review*, May–June (2000): 52–7.

49 Lorien Holland, "From Famine to Feast," *Far Eastern Economic Review*, June 10 (1999), pp. 74–6.

50 We thank Ajantha Suriyanarayanan for this reference in her term paper "The Influence of Corporate Organizations on Cultures through Advertising" for a graduate seminar on globalization taught by Xiangming Chen, Fall Semester, 2001.

51 Andrew Ness, "Retail Space to Let," *The China Business Review*, May–June (1999): 44–9.

52 Xiangming Chen's field interview in Shanghai, July 2001.

53 Sassen, *The Global City*, chapter 9.

54 Peter Marcuse and Ronald van Kempen, "Introduction," pp. 1–21 in Peter Marcuse and Ronald van Kempen, eds., *Globalizing Cities: A New Spatial Order?* (Oxford: Blackwell Publishers, 2000).

55 Sassen, *The Global City*.

56 Sanjoy Chakravorty, "From Colonial City to Globalizing City? The Far-from-Complete Spatial Transformation of Calcutta," pp. 56–77 in Peter Marcuse and Ronald van Kempen, *Globalizing Cities*; Luiz cesar de Queiroz Ribeiro and Edward E. Telles, "Rio de Janeiro: Dualization in a Historically Unequal City," pp. 78–94 in Peter Marcuse and Ronald van Kempen, *Globalizing Cities*, p. 82.

57 Field observations and interviews with local residents by Xiangming Chen during his visit to Barcelona, Spain in 2001.

58 Xiangming Chen, "Chicago as a Global City," *Chicago Office*, 1995, pp. 15–20.

59 See Jeffrey D. Morenoff and Marta Tienda, "Underclass Neighborhoods in Temporal and Ecological Perspective," *The Annals of the American Academy of Political and Social Science*, 551 (1997), pp. 59–72.

60 James Miller, "New Skyscraper Rises in Chicago – on Spec," *The Wall Street Journal*, November 18, 1998, p. A16.

61 Mary Ellen Podmolik, "Downtown Spreading Out as Residents Pour In," *Chicago Sun-Times*, May 10, 1998, p. 20A.

62 See Blair Kamin, "Praise It or Raze It?" *Chicago Tribune*, Tempo Section, Febru-

ary 27, 2002, pp. 1, 4.

63   Sharon Zukin, *Landscapes of Power*, pp. 42–4.

64   Rachel Martin. See note 38.

65   *Shanghai Statistical Yearbook 2002*, p. 48; Jizuo Yin, *A Report of Economic Development*, p. 217.

66   Jizuo Yin, chief editor. *Institutional Reform and Social Transition* (in Chinese) (Shanghai: Shanghai Academy of Social Sciences Press, 2001), p. 122.

67   Shanghai Municipal Housing, Land and Resources Administration Bureau, *Shanghai Real Estate Market* (Beijing: China Statistics Press, 2000), p. 98.

68   Andrew Ness, "Shanghai's Property Markets Begin to Converge," *The China Business Review*, September–October (2000): 36–41.

69   *Shanghai Statistical Yearbook 2002*, p. 110.

70   Peter G. Muller, "The Suburban Transformation of the Globalizing American City," *The Annals of the American Academy of Political and Social Science*, 551 (1997): 44–58.

71   Illinois Department of Employment Services data adapted from Lawrence Bury, "Global Suburb? The Growing Importance of Suburban Economic Centers in the Chicago Global Economy," Undergraduate Honors Thesis, Department of Sociology, University of Illinois at Chicago, 1997, supervised by Xiangming Chen.

72   Joel Garreau, *Edge City: Life on the New Frontier* (New York: Doubleday, 1991).

73   See *Chicago Tribune*, "Rich Suburb, Poor Suburb," November 18, 1996, p. 18.

74   Douglas Holt and Bob Merrifield, "Satellite Cities Find New Orbits," *Chicago Tribune*, January 19, 1999, pp. 1, 7.

75   For studies that examined both the internal and external influences on China's spatial development, see Xiangming Chen, "China's City Hierarchy, Urban Policy and Spatial Development in the 1980s," *Urban Studies*, 28, 3 (1991), pp. 341–67; "China's Growing Integration with the Asia-Pacific Economy," pp. 187–217 in Arif Dirlik, ed., *What Is in a Rim? Critical Perspectives on the Pacific Region Idea* (Lanham, MD: Rowman & Littlefield Publishers, 1998); Xiangming Chen and William Parish, "Urbanization in China: Reassessing an Evolving Model," pp. 61–90 in Josef Gugler, ed., *The Urban Transformation of the Developing World* (Oxford: Oxford University Press, 1996).

76   These indicators were derived and calculated from State Statistical Bureau, *Urban Statistical Yearbook of China 2000* (Beijing: China Statistics Press, 2001), pp. 505–52.

77   See George C. S. Lin, "Metropolitan Development in a Transitional Socialist Economy: Spatial Restructuring in the Pearl River Delta, China," *Urban Studies*, 38, 3 (2001): 383–406; "Evolving Spatial Form of Urban-Rural Interaction in the Pearl River Delta, China," *Professional Geographer*, 53, 1 (2001): 56–70.

78   Also see Peter Dicken, Philip F. Kelly, Kris Olds, and Henry Wai-Chung Yeung, "Chains and Networks, Territories and Scales: Towards a Relational Framework for Analysing the Global Economy," *Global Networks*, 1, 2 (2001): 89–112.

79   See Kyoung-Ho Shin and Michael Timberlake, "World Cities in Asia: Cliques, Centrality and Connectedness," *Urban Studies*, 37, 12 (2000): 2257–85.

80   Jon Van, "Chicago May Net Another 'World's Busiest Designation," *Chicago Tribune*, March 14, 1999, Business Section, p. 1.

81 David Young, "Chicago Still Main Axle of Nation's Railroads," *Chicago Tribune*, November 13, 1996, Business Section, p. 1.

82 See Richard O'Brien, *Global Financial Integration: The End of Geography* (London: The Royal Institute of International Affairs, 1992).

83 See Xiangming Chen, *As Borders Crumble: Transborder Flows and Subregional Formations on the Western Pacific Rim* (Lanham, MD: Rowman & Littlefield Publishers, forthcoming in 2004), ch. 6.

84 See David Harvey, *The Condition of Postmodernity*, p. 44.

85 See Michael Peter Smith, *Transnational Urbanism: Locating Globalization* (Malden, MA: Blackwell Publishers, 2001), p. 5.

CHAPTER FIVE

From a Critical Sociology to a Reconstructive Sociology of Cities

Our overarching themes in this book have been twofold. First, we have examined the nature of place and argued that cities must be seen as places that are essential to human well-being. Second, we have argued that cities also must be seen as significant spaces that both produce and are produced by the social institutions that men and women construct. Here, in this last chapter, we want to press forward with these themes, especially with the ways that cities might be improved given that, as places, they are so critical and fundamental to the lives of humans.

A great deal of the writing today about urban places takes a critical stance toward such sites. Some of the most exciting and popular writing, for instance, that of Mike Davis on Los Angeles, portrays the constraints and limitations of urban places, especially the ways in which business and government impinge upon and limit the freedom of urban residents.[1] Critical thinking of this kind is absolutely essential to our understanding of metropolitan areas for it points to the ways in which the structure of such areas shapes human activity within them. But it is equally important to move beyond such claims in order to reach some understanding, if not agreement, about the manner in which cities might be made better. And that shall be the main task of this chapter. We hope to furnish illustrations of points that, it seems to us, are key to the reconstitution of urban places.

There are a number of ways in which cities can and must be made better. Our emphasis in chapters 3 and 4 on the ways in which social inequalities have become carved into metropolitan space pointed to the difficulties that face many residents, but especially the poor, the black and the recent immigrants, in establishing comfortable and satisfying lives for themselves. Clearly, then, one of the things that one would hope to achieve in creating a reconstruction of urban space is to make a space that is more friendly and inviting to all residents, not simply the rich nor the native white residents. Our reflections and recommendations below, while aimed at the reconstruction of metropolitan space, in general, are very much intended as well to address those matters of inequality that now are evident in so many cities. The reconstruction of place in the city cannot, of course, correct all problems, but it can, at least, point to the ways in which the city can be improved for the most needy who live there.

We begin, then, from our main points laid in the first chapter. Place, we insisted, is something that is of fundamental importance to the nature of human life. It furnishes an anchor to who we are at the same time as it also provides the means for linking ourselves to other human beings. Because of its importance, anything that interferes with the ways in which we are attached to places necessarily interrupts the quality and character of our lives, our essential humanity. If we agree with these premises, then, we must start our search for the ways to reconstruct places by inquiring into the manner in which the connections of people to places, and ultimately to one another, can be made more perfect. It is to that task that we turn first.

Facilitating Attachments to Place

We live in an age, we have noted, when there are continuing contests among major social players for shaping and leaving an imprint on cities. Local government wishes to leave one kind of imprint, whereas global corporations, private developers, or architects, prefer to leave another. When all is said and done, however, in democratic societies that, by definition, declare the rights of citizens and seek to protect and advance those rights, the most important imprint to be left is that of the local residents themselves. But how might this be done when there are so many powerful players engaged in the game of constructing cities and metropolitan areas?

PRO-ACTIVE MEASURES

To foster the sense of community and to nurture the element of personal identity, it is essential, from the outset, that the residents of places possess and exercise the opportunity to shape and to create their own sense of place – to give their own meaning, or meanings, to the places in which they reside – in other words, to leave their special mark on the urban landscape. Though the work of cities must be managed, this does not mean that citizens, seeking to create self-contained communities, cannot pursue such ends to their fullest. Naturally it will be hard to bring such action into full being, especially in the large metropolitan areas that dot the landscapes of so many nations. But there is a way in which such pro-active work can be realized – in the more or less self-contained areas that compose many such cities.

One of the most compelling illustrations today of such democratic work may be discovered in the relatively new ethnic/immigrant communities that have been created over the past thirty years or so. Even though many such communities are, to all outward appearances, places of poverty and despair, in fact, when looked at from the point of view of the residents, they are often thriving and vital sites, *real places in which real people actively are engaged in creating and sustaining the life of one another as of the life of the place*. These newly emergent enclaves help to show how groups of people, frequently lacking in material resources, can nevertheless create for themselves a strong sense of place and, in the course of so doing, a strong sense of themselves and their community. Immigrant enclaves also reveal that powerful places can be established within central cities, not merely on the affluent suburban fringes of metropolitan areas.

CREATING PLACE ANEW

Across the United States today, but also in a number of other countries, such as England, France and Germany, one may find an abundance of immigrant enclaves, groups of people who, coming from the same country, often even from the same villages and towns, have established a new residence, a new habitat, for themselves. Many of these newly-constructed areas depend upon the creation of a strong sense of place, abetted by ways of facilitating ties among the residents of those places by, among other things, establishing new social and civic organizations.

In New York City, for instance, one can find the large Puerto Rican *barrio* as well as major communities of West Indian immigrants. In San Francisco, Chicago and even in London, one can find a variety of Chinatowns, most marked by the large decorative entrance gates, housing a number of restaurants that cater both to local residents and to outsiders, and surviving on an array of keen business skills and a continuing supply of new immigrants. The various forms of Chinatown are especially illustrative of the process whereby new residents create a home for themselves in a metropolitan area because their features are so very visible and prominent.

However, some of the most powerful illustrations of the creation of place by immigrants take the form of the Mexican enclaves. Though there has been a continuing flow of immigrants entering America from Mexico that dates back to the 1920s, at least, the 1965 Immigration Act effectively opened the gates to a flood of new arrivals. By 2000, Mexican residents in the United

States represented the majority of the foreign-born and in cities such as Chicago and Los Angeles they were, far and away, the largest contingent of the immigrant population.

Still, it would be a mistake to think that it is their numbers, alone, that makes the recent Mexican immigrants such a powerful presence. It is not. Instead it is what Mexican immigrants bring to America and the ways in which they reshape the places in which they reside. In effect, they create and remake old American landscapes out of the material of their own history and culture. In cities that range from Milwaukee to San Francisco, the presence of the Mexican immigrants is made immediately visible by the wall murals and public art that adorn their enclaves. Such art traces its origins to the period of the 1920s and 1930s in Mexico, a time during which art became, under the influence of the Mexican artists, Diego Rivera, David Alfaro Siqueiros, and José Clemente Orozco, among others, a way to give vision to the will and energies of the people, *la gente*. Rivera designed dozens of wall murals that, in one way or another, proclaim the dignity of the poor peasants, on the one hand, and declare their anger and outrage at the forces of the military, the government and big capitalism, on the other. Today some of the murals still may be found scattered throughout public buildings in Mexico City, even in public structures in the United States, like that of the University of San Francisco.[2]

What many Mexican immigrant communities have enacted, under the will and instruction of many artists, is to create their own brand of such public murals, or wall art. The wall murals tell a variety of stories of the Mexican people, ranging from myths that date back to the period of the Aztecs, to those that simply celebrate the lives of the contemporary Mexican family. For example, in the Pilsen area of Chicago, located just west of the downtown Loop area, there is a very famous mural, along the northern boundary of the community, that shows an array of fifteen different warriors, representing different branches and attitudes both of Mexicans and of Mexican-Americans. What is so obviously striking about the mural is that its warriors are placed there to stand guard and to protect the residents of the community. First painted in the mid-1970s, under the tutelage of the artist, Aurelio Diaz, it has since been updated by the contributions of a number of other artists and local residents.

Sometimes the wall murals portray images that are extraordinarily powerful. One such mural lies on a major thoroughfare in the Mission District of San Francisco, an area that houses former citizens of Mexico and several other Latin American nations. This particular image (plate 5.3) shows a young child, school briefcase tucked under his arm, being protected from the guns of war by a large pair of hands stretched out before him. A mural conveying a somewhat similar image may be found above the entrance to the Pius VI School in Pilsen. This particular mural (plate 5.4) shows the two

Plates 5.1 and 5.2   Galerio del Bario in Pilsen District, Chicago.

Mexican symbols, of the eagle and the bear, standing on either side of and protecting an assembled family as it turns the pages of an open book. Obviously the mural is intended to illustrate the importance of education, and of the family, in the pursuit of such a goal for the Mexican community. It stands as an ideal, a constant reminder to the members of the community, of the importance of education and, of course, of the importance of their cultural heritage.

Yet the wall murals are only the most obvious and outward presence of the ways in which the Mexican immigrants have remade the dying core of many American cities. The full cultural and social presence of the Mexicans may be discovered elsewhere, in the markets that have been created, markets that often resemble those of Mexico and, at the same time, serve as the conveyance for the sale of Mexican imports in the United States. So, too, the cultural presence of Mexicans is made evident in their worship, particularly in the wide array of Catholic churches that dot many Mexican enclaves. Civic and social organizations also are an integral part of these new communities, some fashioned to pursue political goals on behalf of their residents, others to help secure housing for many people who are otherwise unable to secure it for themselves.

In brief, what happens in such self-contained communities is that their residents create over a period of time a place in which they feel comfortable – and, most of all, at home. And they do so, in effect, by creating and recreat-

Plate 5.3   Image of child in Mission District, San Francisco.

Plate 5.4   St. Pius V School mural in Pilsen District, Chicago.

ing elements of their homelands. Sometimes it is an easy process for, coming from the same *pueblos* of Mexico, they simply awake to a different geographic and national presence. They make a place for themselves; they establish the institutional foundations for the continuing vitality of their community; they manufacture the elements necessary for their own security; by reshaping the material environment they have found at hand. None of this is to deny the many impediments and burdens faced by the people living in such areas. They are of enormous proportions, frequently debilitating the energies of residents. But, if truth be told, they are only one part of a much larger story.

CELEBRATING PLACE/COMMUNITY

Another way in which the attachment of people to places can be fostered is through the deliberate efforts, often sponsored and promoted by the larger metropolis, to celebrate the idea of community. Such efforts have the effect of reminding residents of the history of the place in which they reside as well as how the groups, or communities, of which they are a part, represent an essential piece of those places. In recent times, cities across the United States have made efforts to celebrate themselves with a variety of activities, all of which are designed to reinforce the identity of those places, while, sometimes unintentionally, reinforcing the place-attachments of residents.

In Milwaukee, Wisconsin, for instance, there is a summer festival that brings together people from across the city and sites well beyond. Summer Fest is designed to celebrate the history of the city, in part simply by bringing people together for a variety of amusements and different kinds of local foods to eat. In Chicago, a similar kind of celebration takes place in the form of a two-week festival, Taste of Chicago. The rich heritage of the city and the large appetites of residents are celebrated at one and the same time: it becomes a device for revealing the diverse ethnic make-up and heritage of the city, and doing so in a single downtown site, Grant Park, where everyone is forced to commingle. The effect, of course, is literally to bring people together, frequently from neighborhoods that are miles apart in distance and classes apart in wealth, doing so under the banner of the city itself.

Countless other similar events are held in the form of parades, road races, parties, and other festive events held in many cities throughout America. A number of cities, for example, sponsor various kinds of runs and bike races, many of them designed to raise money for charitable events but that also serve the larger purpose of reminding people of the place in which they live. In addition, some major metropolitan areas, like New York, Chicago, Philadelphia and Detroit, hold annual parades that promote the heritage of specific ethnic/immigrant communities within them. New York City, for instance, holds a major parade in the early summer to celebrate the heritage of its Puerto Rican residents, while Chicago holds a variety of major parades throughout the year, from the one in early March, to honor St. Patrick, to the Bud Billiken parade, that honors a major black figure, to the various ethnic heritage and neighborhood ensembles sprinkled across June, July, and August.

Besides such festivals, and celebrations, there are the more deliberate and focused efforts to protect and to preserve the actual historical record of the city. As the nation has aged, more and more preservationist groups have emerged in America. Often they direct their attention to ensuring that no historic site be torn down, using the authority of the federal laws that uphold historic preservation. The homes of founding figures in local sites may be preserved as well. Though perhaps too little is done of this in American cities – indeed, far more is conserved in Europe, for example, than in the United States – the effort is nevertheless important precisely because the historical record, assembled in documents, reminds people of a key reality to their lives, that of the overarching city/metropolis itself. Indeed, to the degree that such efforts fail, frequently because of the success of an affluent developer in convincing a local city government of the great gains to be had from new construction, the sense of place can be lost and, with it, an anchor to the identity and community among people.

The urban planner and architectural historian, Dolores Hayden, who teaches at Yale University, has developed a major public project whose broad purpose is to preserve the history and the integrity of places in the city. Beginning in the early 1980s, Hayden formed a group, "The Power of Place," which works directly with various residents and neighborhood organizations in Los Angeles, California to preserve the records of specific places within the city.[3] This project is intended to help "situate women's history and ethnic history . . . in public places . . . through experimental collaboration projects by historians, designers and artists."[4] The group's preservation projects have ranged from documenting the existence of produce and flower markets to saving historical records about various immigrants and workers in Los Angeles.

Now one might, of course, dismiss these efforts as merely superficial, the piecemeal attempts by local governments or even prominent historians, to give marginal groups "their day in the sun." But we maintain, to the contrary, that such efforts to celebrate place are very vital to the sense of community that comes to be shared by people. Regular festive occasions, whether road races or rich servings of ethnic dishes, help to cement in the minds of local citizens the significance of the communities to which they belong. They revive and restore the community, doing so, in part, by actually bringing members of the community together in a specific site. They are social rituals that are part of the everyday fabric of community life, as Emile Durkheim so long ago informed us.[5] And, because they are so, it is important both to the life of the place and to the lives of its citizens that they be carried forward and maintained.

PROMOTING LOCAL SOCIAL ACTIVITY

In her seminal work about cities, *The Death and Life of Great American Cities*, Jane Jacobs argued that cities must be designed in such a way as to promote daily activity and social intercourse among residents.[6] In part, she was reacting to the then-fashion among the modernist urban planners and architects to design cities that were perhaps aesthetically attractive but devoid of all arrangements that would facilitate social interaction. She wrote, for example, of concrete sites, like sidewalks and streets:

> The trust of a city street is formed over time from many, many little public sidewalk contacts. It grows out of people stopping by at the bar for a beer, getting advice from the grocer and giving advice to the newsstand man, comparing opinions with other customers at the bakery and nodding hello to the two boys drinking pop on the stoop, eying the girls while waiting to be called for dinner, admonishing the children, hearing about a job from the hardware man and borrowing a dollar from the druggist, admiring the new babies and sympathizing over the way a coat faded. . . . The sum of such casual, public contact at a local level . . . is a feeling for the public identity of a people, a web of public respect and trust, and a resource in time of personal or neighborhood need. *The absence of this trust is a disaster to a city street.* (Our emphasis)[7]

Jacobs insisted that such activity was vital to the life of the city and, especially, to the lives of its residents. She argued that every effort must be taken by planners and architects and city officials to build structures and cities that encouraged the easy social activities and exchanges among people.

That theme, which was central to her analysis and has influenced subsequent generations of urban thinkers, can be found in a variety of quarters today. It is an essential building block in the effort to foster the attachment of people to places and to one another. In neighborhoods, for example, there have been in recent years a number of organized efforts that, in advancing the interests of the neighborhood, work to foster common and cooperative social relations among its residents. Suburban neighborhoods can be attractive but also socially isolating. Individual property owners may possess large and wonderful yards, but the ambience has been such as to discourage much in the way of neighborly contact. However, homeowners associations, often constructed as a defense against the real or imagined onslaughts of developers, have had the effect of bringing people together and making them work on common activities. They thus advance the sense of place by advancing the sense of community.

Another way in which the connections of people to places and to one another can be fostered is through the adequate provision of public areas where people can gather and assemble together easily. The very purpose of the early park system in the United States, for example, was to furnish a kind of refuge and leisure space for local residents, a site in which they could enjoy themselves, having picnics or their children play at large. Moreover, cities like London and Paris historically have built major park systems, making these public spaces freely available to all local citizens. On warm summer evenings, such parks swell with the numbers of people, many engaged in a diversity of activities, from simply strolling the paths to sitting alongside the ponds and fountains in the parks. Such facilities provide not simply recreation but the unintended consequence of bringing people together in the same place, allowing them to socialize and to identify with the larger place itself.

Along similar lines, open-air public markets often serve the same function as parks, bringing a large and often diverse population of people together. Cities like London historically have had a variety of such public markets, including the well-known Petticoat Lane in the East End, and the newer public markets in Brixton (see plates 5.5 and 5.6). In such areas, one can find a wide variety of goods and stores. People mingle and shop together, and many do so on a regular daily basis. The effect, again, is to promote social connectedness among people. Some American cities have taken up a similar venture, providing public markets where people can come to shop and spend time in the company of one another. Markets can be found in cities as diverse as New York, Portland, Santa Fe, and Minneapolis.

Plates 5.5 and 5.6   Brixton markets, London.

The main point of all this work of design and planning is basically to promote on a regular basis the social connections of people. By setting aside specific public sites, even by designing new villages to be small and compact, urban planners can have a positive and important impact on the way people come to feel about places. If they associate their own well-being with the quality of social life in a place, so much the better, for such activity will make that specific place, in the here and now, essential to the lives of those residents. Concrete, or real, places do not have to be particularly beautiful or materially abundant to be important to the lives of human beings. They simply must be designed in such a way as to enhance the natural connections between people and places.

Protective Measures

Just as one must take pro-active steps to facilitate the attachments of people to places, so, too, one must take some protective measures as well. The two powerhouses that often infringe on the rights of local residents to leave their own mark on places are those of business and government. Business is most often the biggest offender of all.

BUSINESS

Business has always had a major impact on the shaping of the metropolis, whether in the form of the work of real estate developers or bankers that control the mortgages available to local residents (see above, also chapter 1). In recent years, but especially since the early 1970s, national and international economic forces have come to play a special part in shaping the landscape of cities. Bankers and telecommunication companies, with international ties and markets, offer priceless advantages to cities, especially in the form of new employment and other financial rewards. Such companies thus have been pursued aggressively by a variety of cities (see chapter 4). But in the process such forces also have altered the distribution of wealth in the local community, in particular, helping to fuel a bifurcation of the city, between the high-end wealthy sector and the low-end service sector. The effect has been, according to some analysts, to also shape the landscape of cities, producing affluent residences almost side-by-side impoverished sections of the city.

Given the profound impact that business continues to have, then, over the shape of the city, what might be done to temper its influence, especially in the sense that it appears to heighten and sharpen the social and economic inequalities in cites? So far there are some obvious though limited steps that can be taken. One, of course, is simply the form of local homeowners associations. Such associations, as we have already noted, act to protect the interests of homeowners largely by stymieing efforts of developers, and their allies, to take over and develop property in specific areas of the city. Another step is, as the city of Santa Monica did a few years ago, to compel businesses and developers to set aside public lands for the use of citizens in return for certain tax and economic incentives that the developers receive from the city.[8] This obviously represents an important measure because of the significance of public space to the life of the city and its residents.

But apart from these limited measures, what precisely can local residents do to ward off the deleterious effects of business, especially of the global businesses that do appear to heighten economic inequalities within the city? This is the central question that so many citizens ponder today. There are the radical efforts, of course. These are evident in the various social movements that have assembled in recent months to march against, sometimes to wage war against, the great global economic forces, such as the International Monetary Fund and the group of G-8 nations of the world. Some of these movements are primarily efforts at reform. They might seek, for example, simply to ensure that the environment is not put in further jeopardy by the increase in industrialization, and its byproducts, across the world. Some wage a campaign on behalf of health remedies, especially for the devastating pandemic of AIDS that has swept across Africa, leaving tens of millions of people dead or in imminent danger of death. The success of such movements, however far removed their goals might be from those of local residents, can nevertheless help to deter the unrestrained growth and intrusion of global capitalism in various nations and metropolitan areas.

For local residents, it is essential that they not only organize to protect neighborhoods, but that they organize to ensure that the local political officials are both powerful and enlightened, with a vision of the metropolitan future that does not simply include bringing in as much global enterprise as possible. True, new companies help cities, especially those that have recently crept out from under the declines of dying industries. New industry does bring new jobs, but sometimes the jobs are only for the very well trained and educated – the top-flight computer experts or bankers – or, at the other end, for merely unskilled labor. Such industry does tend to further bifurcate the population into the rich and poor without necessarily adding to the skills and wealth of the middle-class.

Accordingly, local political leaders must be selective in the kinds of enterprises they recruit. They must seek to bring in cutting-edge technology companies, but not tie their future only to such firms. The "dot.com" crashes and the decline in the technology industry in early 2001 left certain metropolitan areas, like Austin, Texas, in difficult straits, primarily because modern Austin had tied its own metropolitan fortunes so much to the expansion and growth of companies like Dell Computers and various software firms. Even cities like San Francisco have suffered through such recent declines as well. Somehow local political leaders must possess a vision that balances the benefits that can result from bringing in new business enterprises at the same time that it works hard to produce material benefits for the working class; total wealth must be balanced against helping the poor, in other words. In addition, in this age and time, there must be a determined effort as well to lessen the difficult journey to American shores of the new immigrants. Many of these immigrants are the grit and muscle of the modern economy, working in low-skill jobs, gardening, landscaping, helping in restaurants, often with the common aim of improving their own lives.

Local leaders, we would maintain, can make a difference, as can local cities – like the Portland, Oregons, or Minneapolis, Minnesotas of the world. And to see further how such cities and their officials can make a difference let us now turn to consider more carefully how government can shape the future of places.

GOVERNMENT

Though government in a democratic society is, in principle, intended to aid and abet the wishes of the majority of citizens, often, of course, it fails to do so. Indeed, as cities seek to improve and to enhance themselves, government becomes a key partner with business, seeking in whatever manner to secure their good fortune by securing the fortunes of businesses, themselves. Local governments provide a variety of devices to encourage new business, including various forms of tax incentives and other strategic financial breaks.

Only enlightened leadership, then, of local government can have an impact, and show the way both to limit the effects of business and to promote the interests of local residents at the same time. Today one prominent effort in this direction is that of **regionalism**. It is the effort on the part of local legislators to broaden the scope of local government and to diminish the wide gaps that exist in the public resources available to the poor as compared to the affluent areas of the metropolis.

In principle, **regionalism** represents an attempt to coordinate the services available from government to the various residential and commercial sectors of the metropolis. As we noted earlier, in chapter 3, historically in the United States great divisions have grown up between the central cities and the suburbs, divisions in terms of the income of residents as well as their racial and ethnic backgrounds. Because property taxes provide the means whereby localities get much of their work done, such as fire and police services, utilities and, most important of all, schools, the division has meant that the wealthier white areas typically get the best services. Regionalism attempts to combat this sort of problem by trying to provide greater equity in the use of public resources for such things as schools as well as utilities. Moreover, in some places, like Minneapolis, and under the inspired leadership of former Congressman Myron Orfield, regionalism has been taken even further.[9] Using the Metropolitan Council, a regional body created in Minneapolis in 1967, as well as forging a coalition between the city and the representatives of older suburbs, Orfield has been able to push for low-income housing in affluent areas, thereby trying to reduce some of the economic inequalities. But there remain tremendous obstacles to implementing the goals of regionalism, especially among the many municipal governments that seek to retain their autonomy and control over their own finances and populations.

Regionalism, of course, is not a policy pursued only in the United States but it is pursued in Europe as well, primarily in the new European Union but also in more local efforts that try to bring together public and administrative services for regions of different countries. The great advantage of a regional program is that it can help ease some of the historic social and economic inequalities in areas by trying to furnish more balanced and equitable public resources. The ultimate goal, of course, is to furnish some kind of redistribution of wealth so that the sharp differences between the poor and the rich can be ameliorated through the political work of places.

Summary

We have covered much territory in our discussion here about the ways both to facilitate attachment to place and to protect the interests of local residents, particularly the poor, in places. Most of all, it is important that every effort be made to remind local residents of the significance of place to their lives, to try at all costs to make more secure the natural bonds between the quality of life of human beings and the significance that place has for their lives. As the pace of the world increases, as globalism spills its products over into local arenas, of course it will be more of a challenge to make these links between place and the lives of residents enduring ones. We hope, however, that in this section we have pointed at least in the direction of first measures.

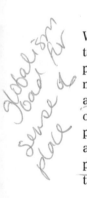

The urban vision of architects and urban planners: The New Urbanism and the construction of neo-traditional places

Our concerns here in this book, about the importance of place to the lives of human beings, are, it turns out, also evident in the work of a number of modern urban planners, architects, and environmentalists. One of the first voices to raise the issue about the significance of place in modern America was the writer, James Howard Kunstler. Kunstler spoke not of the meaning of place, but rather the meaninglessness of places in modern America – that every place looked like every other place and therefore, each place was no place at all. "To me," he writes, "[America] is a landscape of scary places, the geography of nowhere, that has simply ceased to be a credible human habitat."[10]

Over the past two decades a movement has grown up that tries to take these theoretical concerns and criticisms about real places in America today and turn them into a vision (or visions) for actually creating new villages and towns, remaking older urban areas, and, in general, rehabilitating the American residential/workplace landscape. Although it has been criticized as offering very little in the way of new ideas, this movement, which has become known as the **New Urbanism** (it has its own organization, the Congress of the New Urbanism, with the website, www.cnu.org), has plucked certain ideas from the past, as in the work of the Garden City designed by Ebenezer Howard, and added its own particular twists to the new town setting. Under the inspiration of architects and planners, in particular, Peter Calthorpe, Andres Duany and Elizabeth Plater-Zyberk, the New Urbanism proposes a model of the city and region that attempts to integrate issues of transportation, landscape, environment and organization into a new form of the smaller integrated community.[11]

It focuses much of its attention on the person as pedestrian. Much of the concern of the New Urbanists has to do with the problems created by automobiles, and the vast highway system, for the residential space of Americans. Accordingly, spaces are designed, for example, by Duany and Plater-Zyberk, that are no more than one-quarter mile in length, the distance that can be traversed by the average person in about five or ten minutes. Within this quarter mile, space is laid out for central transportation agencies, such as trains, as well as for common grounds and local shopping areas. Such areas are designed to promote the pedestrian traffic of people, to trains that will take them to work or to stores where they can shop. In addition, the large commons areas are intended to provide recreational space for many residents, thus furnishing a site where people can gather and get to know their neighbors.

The central principles of the New Urbanists are laid out in a document on their website (see chart 5.1).

The work of the New Urbanists continues to evolve, particularly in the visions of people like Calthorpe. In his most recent book, Calthorpe and co-author William Fulton, write of the "regional city," a city that is designed as part and parcel of an integrated area.[12] The region is built on concerns with the ecology of the area, in terms of such matters as an area's watershed; the demography of the area, in terms of specific limits on density and growth; the equity among the residents, calling for such things as affordable housing and a redistribution of tax revenues so that wealthier suburbs do not simply soak up all the public benefits; and the transportation of the region, encouraging greater public transportation and more limited use of expressways. The region, moreover, is designed to revolve around the central hub of a city, but includes outlying suburban areas as well; and it is also designed not only to promote the growth of new areas, but to redevelop the older central city sites, too.

Chart 5.1
Charter of the New
Urbanism

The Congress for the New Urbanism views disinvestment in central cities, the spread of placeless sprawl, increasing separation by race and income, environmental deterioration, loss of agricultural lands and wilderness, and the erosion of society's built heritage as one interrelated community-building challenge.

We stand for the restoration of existing urban centers and towns within coherent metropolitan regions, the reconfiguration of sprawling suburbs into communities of real neighborhoods and the diverse districts, the conservation of natural environments, and the preservation of our built legacy.

We recognize that physical solutions by themselves will not solve social and economic problems, but neither can economic vitality, community stability, and environmental health be sustained without a coherent and supportive physical framework.

We advocate the restructuring of public policy and development practices to support the following principles: neighborhoods should be diverse in use and population; communities should be designed for the pedestrian and transit as well as the car; cities and towns should be shaped by physically defined and universally accessible public spaces and community institutions; urban places should be framed by architecture and landscape design that celebrate local history, climate, ecology, and building practice.

We represent a broad-based citizenry, composed of public and private sector leaders, community activists, and multidisciplinary professionals. We are committed to reestablishing the relationship between the art of building and the making of community, through citizen-based participatory planning and design.

We dedicate ourselves to reclaiming our homes, blocks, streets, parks, neighborhoods, districts, towns, cities, regions, and environment.

We assert the following principles to guide public policy, development practice, urban planning, and design:

THE REGION: METROPOLIS, CITY AND TOWN

1   *Metropolitan regions are finite places with geographic boundaries derived from topography, watersheds, coastlines, farmlands, regional parks, and river basins. The metropolis is made of multiple centers that are cities, towns, and villages, each with its own identifiable centre and edges.*

2   *The metropolitan region is a fundamental economic unit of the contemporary world. Governmental cooperation, public policy, physical planning, and economic strategies must reflect this new reality.*

3   *The metropolis has a necessary and fragile relationship to its agrarian hinterland and natural landscapes. The relationship is environmental, economic and cultural. Farmland and nature are as important to the metropolis as the garden is to the house.*

4   *Development patterns should not blur or eradicate the edges of the metropolis. Infill development within existing urban areas conserves environmental resources, economic investment, and social fabric, while reclaiming marginal and abandoned areas. Metropolitan regions should develop strategies to encourage such infill development over peripheral expansion.*

5   *Where appropriate, new development contiguous to urban boundaries should be organized as neighborhoods and districts, and be integrated with the existing urban pattern. Noncontiguous development should be organized as towns and village with their own urban edges, and planned for a jobs/housing balance, not as bedroom suburbs.*

6   *The development and redevelopment of towns and cities should respect historical patterns, precedents, and boundaries.*

7   *Cities and towns should bring into proximity a broad spectrum of public and private uses to support a regional economy that benefits people of all income. Affordable housing should be distributed throughout the region to match job opportunities and to avoid concentrations of poverty.*

8   *The physical organization of the region should be supported by a framework of transportation alternatives. Transit, pedestrian, and bicycle systems should maximize access and mobility throughout the region while reducing dependence upon the automobile.*

9   *Revenues and resources can be shared more cooperatively among the municipalities and centers within regions to avoid destructive competition for tax base and to promote rational coordination of transportation, recreation, public services, housing, and community institutions.*

THE NEIGHBORHOOD, THE DISTRICT AND THE CORRIDOR

1   *The neighborhood, the district, and the corridor are the essential elements of development and redevelopment in the metropolis. They form indentifiable areas that encourage citizens to take responsibility for their maintenance and evolution.*

2   *Neighborhoods should be compact, pedestrian-friendly, and mixed-use. Districts gener-*

ally emphasize a special single use, and should follow the principles of neighborhood design when possible. Corridors are regional connectors of neighborhoods and districts; they range from boulevards and rail lines to rivers and parkways.

3   Many activities of daily living should occur within walking distance, allowing independence to those who do not drive, especially the elderly and the young. Interconnected networks of streets should be designed to encourage walking, reduce the number and length of automobile trips, and conserve energy.

4   Within neighborhoods, a broad range of housing types and price levels can bring people of diverse ages, races, and incomes into daily interaction, strengthening the personal and civic bonds essential to an authentic community.

5   Transit corridors, when properly planned and coordinated, can help organize metropolitan structure and revitalize urban centers. In contrast, highway corridors should not displace investment from existing centers.

6   Appropriate building densities and land uses should be within walking distance of transit stops, permitting public transit to become a viable alternative to the automobile.

7   Concentrations of civic, institutional, and commercial activity should be embedded in neighborhoods and districts, not isolated in remote, single-use complexes. Schools should be sized and located to enable children to walk or bicycle to them.

8   The economic health and harmonious evolution of neighborhoods, districts, and corridors can be improved through graphic urban design codes that serve a predictable guides for change.

9   A range of parks, from tot-lots and village greens to ballfields and community gardens, should be distributed within neighborhoods. Conservation areas and open lands should be used to define and connect different neighborhoods and districts.

THE BLOCK, THE STREET, AND THE BUILDING

1   A primary task of all urban architecture and landscape design is the physical definition of streets and public spaces as places of shared use.

2   Individual architectural projects should be seamlessly linked to their surroundings. This issue transcends style.

3   The revitalization of urban places depends on safety and security. The design of streets and buildings should reinforce safe environments, but not at the expense of accessibility and openness.

4   In the contemporary metropolis, development must adequately accommodate automobiles. It should do so in ways that respect the pedestrian and the form of public space.

5   Streets and squares should be safe, comfortable, and interesting to the pedestrian. Properly configured, they encourage walking and enable neighbors to know each other and protect their communities.

6   Architecture and landscape design should grow from local climate, topography, history, and building practice.

7   Civic buildings and public gathering places require important sites to reinforce community identity and the culture of democracy. They deserve distinctive form, because their role is different from that of other buildings and places that constitute the fabric of the city.

8   All buildings should provide their inhabitants with a clear sense of location, weather and time. Natural methods of heating and cooling can be more resource-efficient than mechanical systems.

9   Preservation and renewal of historic buildings, districts, and landscapes affirm the continuity and evolution of urban society.

For information: Congress for the New Urbanism; 5 Third Street, Suite 725, San Francisco, CA 94103 Phone: 415 495-2255 Fax: 415 495-1731

There are several prominent examples of the kind of villages and regions designed by New Urbanists. One of the most famous of all is that of Seaside, Florida, designed by Duany and Plater-Zyberk and completed in 1983. This is the place where the movie "The Truman Show," starring Jim Carey, was filmed. It is somewhat ironic that this movie took place there because the point of the movie is that Truman has grown up in a totally manufactured environment, nothing of which is real but rather the construction of a television crew that has followed Truman's life from its first day. Notice, in the pictures, how narrow the streets are and the porches found on almost every house. The purpose of the narrow streets is to eliminate most car traffic, porches to encourage a friendly sociable atmosphere, and the small distances equally to bring people together. The basic notion is that by making such villages people/pedestrian friendly, individuals will become more readily connected to the places in which they live.

A number of other illustrations exist of the New Urbanist principles, including the West Laguna Beach area in California, and Kentlands in Maryland. Calthorpe, in his latest book, uses Portland, Oregon to illustrate his notion of a regional city. Portland, in fact, has become the darling of the progressive urbanists, largely because it has developed a set of laws to guide planning in the metropolitan region. And, among other things, it has developed an urban growth boundary, which limits the amount of growth that may take place beyond the boundary and into more rural and farmland areas.

The New Urbanist paradigm has been criticized on several grounds. One is that it is not really new so much as eclectic, drawing on a variety of past principles. Along similar lines, others argue that it is hopelessly attached to a much earlier time in American history, when it was possible for people to reside in small, village-like places. Critics say that the New Urbanist vision is not practical for a nation the scale of modern America. A third criticism is that it seems largely designed for an affluent population of people who can afford to live in these smaller utopian communities and who can travel to work by train. In response to this, it appears, some New Urbanists are intent on creating a vari-

Plate 5.7 Overhead view of Seaside, Florida. Photo © Alex S. Maclean.

Plate 5.8 Street of homes leading to Atlantic Ocean in Seaside, Florida. Photo © Steven M. Brooke.

Plate 5.9 Gazebo and residents in Seaside, Florida. Photo © Steven M. Brooke.

ety of residences in their villages, residences that vary by income level and that can include smaller houses as well as rental units attached to larger places.

Yet, despite such criticisms, there is one major strength of the New Urban vision – it offers a way to think about cities and regions from a larger perspective, and that it makes every effort to build places that will accommodate the social needs of their residents. To us these are key principles for the design and redesign of places.

Remaking human habitats across the world

It is, of course, one matter to think about how to reconstruct American cities in such a way that they are more inviting to their residents, and that they encourage a greater attachment to place by people. The New Urbanists have at least furnished a kind of vision to pursue in thinking about how we can improve the lives of people who reside in metropolitan areas at the beginning of the twenty-first century. And yet, it is an entirely separate issue when we think about residence, and work and life, for the tens of millions of people who live in desperate and impoverished circumstances in so many nations of the world.

Who cares about patterns of sociability when, in fact, people are starving daily where one lives? Who really needs to be concerned with the issues of regional ecology when the land has been devastated by drought, and the population ravaged by AIDS, sometimes by civil wars? Much effort must be put into providing housing and shelter for the millions of people who now live on the fringes of the metropolis in Africa, Latin America, and Asia. There are concerns and needs that are worlds apart from those we experience in the United States. And, leading in the effort to provide both information and inspiration in this effort is the work of the United Nations Centre for Human Settlements.

The United Nations has provided a regular series of reports on the concentrations of people in urban areas across the world over the past decade or so, holding major conferences and publishing, as they did this year, a report on the issue of urbanization across the world. *Cities in a Globalizing World* provides an array of various statistics, on housing and income, for the many populations of urban dwellers throughout the world.[13] In addition, it also furnishes a number of specific reports dealing with pressing topics, primarily the impact of "globalization" on metropolitan areas, and how local places, and their residents, can seek to improve the living conditions within them. Most of the effort in many of these places must be devoted to dealing simply with the matter of poverty, on the one hand, and AIDS, and its devastation, on the other. Beyond those major issues, however, cities across the world face somewhat similar problems: how to deal with the inequalities within the metropolitan region; how to effect a better system of governance when global forces so easily intrude on local ones; and how to involve citizens, in a regular and active fashion, in deciding the policies necessary to their own fate and that of their fellow residents.

To all of these, there are no easy answers, as the UN Report documents. But it does lay out the challenges, challenges that must be faced today and met tomorrow. Just as the New Urbanists have tried to combat the issues of too many cars and too little attention to the environment, the proponents of the UN program seek to deal with the varying nature of metropolitan living across the world. Clearly housing is a central issue, and must be resolved for those millions who live on the fringes of the metropolis in squatter settlements. Health is an equally important issue, and must be faced head on if the quality of life in the metropolis in the twenty-first century is to be decent.

These are challenges that must be taken as personal ones by all of us. And, mainly, by those of us who are young and concerned with the fabric of the city. It is among this generation that solutions will be invented and found, ones that can help everyone, but especially the poor and the minorities, to aspire and to succeed to a better urban life in the future. Let us all work hard to make the cities of the world into better places!

Notes

1   Mike Davis, *City of Quartz: Excavating the Future in Los Angeles* (London: Verso, 1990); *The Ecology of Fear: Los Angeles and the Imagination of Disaster* (New York: Metropolitan Books, 1998).

2   Diego Rivera, with Gladys Marsh, *My Art, My Life: An Autobiography.* New York: Dover Publications, 1991.

3   Dolores Hayden, *The Power of Place: Urban Landscapes as Public History* (Cambridge, MA: The MIT Press, 1997).

4   Ibid., p. xi.

5   Emile Durkheim, *The Elementary Forms of the Religious Life*, translated from the French by Joseph Ward Swain (New York: Collier Books, 1961).

6   Jane Jacobs, *The Death and Life of Great American Cities* (New York: Random House, 1961).

7   Ibid., p. 56.

8   Pierre Clavel, *The Progressive City* (New Brunswick, NJ: Rutgers University Press), chapter 5.

9   Myron Orfield, *Metropolitics: A Regional Agenda for Community and Stability* (Washington, DC: The Brookings Institution, and Boston, MA, The Lincoln Institute of Land Policy, 1997).

10 James Howard Kunstler, *The Geography of Nowhere: The Rise and Decline of America's Man-Made Landscape.* (New York: Simon & Schuter, 1993), p.15; see also James Howard Kunstler, *Home from Nowhere: Remaking Our Everyday World for the 21st Century* (New York: Simon & Schuster, 1996).

11 Peter Calthorpe, *The Next American Metropolis: Ecology, Community and the American Dream.* (Princeton: Princeton Architectural Press, 1993); Peter Katz, *The New Urbanism: Toward An Architecture of Community* (New York: McGraw-Hill, 1994); William Fulton, *The New Urbanism: Hope or Hype for American Communities?* (Cambridge, MA: Lincoln Land Institute of Urban Policy, 1996).

12 Peter Calthorpe and William Fulton, *The Regional City: Planning for the End of Sprawl.* (Washington, D.C.: Island Press, 2001).

13 *Cities in A Globalizing World: Global Report on Human Settlements 2001.* United Nations Centre for Human Settlements (Habitat) (London: Earthscan Publications, 2001).

Glossary

Assimilation – the incorporation of immigrants into the life of a host society, it can range from partial, as participation in the economic life of the host society, to complete, which would cover participation in the full range of life, from economic to political to cultural to social.

El Barrio – the enclaves occupied by Latinos, they typically refer to the residential settlements of Puerto Ricans and Mexicans in the United States.

Black metropolis – a term invented by the social scientists, St. Clair Drake and Horace Cayton, to refer to the areas of Chicago's Southside occupied exclusively by African-Americans in the first half of the twentieth century.

Built environment – a term used by urban scholars to refer to all the man-made elements of cities, such as skyscrapers, streets, and other physical infrastructure.

Capital – the resource in the capitalist economic system that is used to produce, transfer, and distribute commodities by and among individual parties and corporate entities.

Capitalism – the dominant economic system in the world today in which property and means of production are controlled by private parties and used by them to create profits under market principles.

Central city – a term that generally refers to the dense central area of a metropolis, where many businesses are located and, in many American cities, the poorer minority residents as well. What is the central city may vary from country to country.

Circuits of capitalism – a term used specifically by such urban scholars as Henri Lefevre, David Harvey and Mark Gottdiener. There are three separate circuits of capitalism: the first circuit, which is that of production; the second circuit, which is that of land and buildings, or real estate; and the third circuit, which is that of scientific knowledge and expertise.

City – an area in which there exists a dense concentration of people, their residential settlements and their forms of economic and social life. Also an area in which there is a dense concentration of capital that helps to promote the concentrations of people and of economic organizations. What is legally and administratively defined as a city varies across countries according to different criteria.

Commodity – the goods produced and distributed under the capitalist economic system, they bear the stamp of the value they carry in the system.

Competition – in the urban context, the term is used by the human ecologists to refer to the processes that exist in the struggle to occupy land and space in the city by different population groups.

Core city – the term used by some scholars, especially world-system theorists, to refer to cities that occupy strategically important positions and thus wield dominant economic functions within the world-system.

Creative destruction – a term originally invented by the economist, Joseph Schumpeter, to refer to the continual replacement of old commodities by new ones under capitalism. Adapted by the urban scholar, Sharon Zukin, to refer to the processes that are constantly refashioning cities.

Dialectic – a term invented by the philosopher, G. W. F. Hegel, and later appropriated by the social theorist, Karl Marx. It refers to the tension and struggle between two competing elements. Such elements can be as different as systems of ideas (Hegel) or social classes (Marx). The key point is that in the process of such struggle, new forms are produced that improve upon and advance the accomplishments of the previous parties. So, for example, in Marx's theory, the struggle between the workers and the capitalists under modern capitalism ultimately would be resolved in a new social form, that of the communist society. The standard way to depict the dialectic is in terms of three elements: (1) thesis versus (2) anti-thesis resolved in (3) synthesis.

Enclave – refers today to the dense, spatially distinctive, self-contained settlements of immigrants or other groups of the same ethnic or minority status or even sociocultural characteristics and lifestyles.

Environment - the material and/or symbolic objects which are external to human beings, and their organizations, and that shape human action and can be shaped by human action in return.

Ethnicity – the common origins of a group of a people, typically rooted in a common national heritage but also at times in a common religious or cultural heritage as well.

Exchange-value – in the theory of Karl Marx, it refers to the value of a commodity when exchanged by its owners for other goods or money in the market.

Gender – the differences that exist between men and women in terms other than physiological or biological ones; typically considered to be socially constructed traits that reflect the values of society.

Global city – a term specifically invented and given to a small number of very large metropolitan areas in modern society by the sociologist, Saskia Sassen. Sassen used the term originally to refer to three cities – London, New York, and Tokyo – which, she claimed, exercised disproportionally great power in the modern world. Such cities have a number of attributes, among them, a highly concentrated core of such producer services as finance, banking, and information processing, as well as a deep and growing inequality between their richer and poorer segments.

Globalization – the primarily economic process that tends to break down national boundaries and barriers and brings countries closer together through trade, investment, and advanced forms of transportation and telecommunications; it is a process, so its proponents claim, that will eventually reshape the full range of human activities.

Growth machine – a concept invented by the sociologist, Harvey Molotch, to refer to cities in the United States. It suggests that cities, and their leaders, are concerned almost exclusively with and pushing for one goal - that of growth, often through an alliance with the business community.

Human ecology – the theory developed and implemented by sociologists at the University of Chicago early in the twentieth century, it proposed to think of cities as sites where various population groups struggled to become dominant. Some groups would win out in the struggle, and thus control certain areas, while other groups would be displaced to less strategic and valuable sites within the city. Human ecology places a strong emphasis on the role of market competition, population growth, technology, and the physical environment in shaping urban life.

Immigration – the movement of people into a new place, either a city or a country. When referring to countries, the place of origin is called the homeland and the place of destination, or resettlement, the host society.

Industrialization – the creation of an economic base rooted in firms and factories that produce goods through the employment of a large labor force and the use of various kinds of heavy equipment and machinery. It depicts the process that took place in many Western countries over the course of the nineteenth and twentieth centuries. It did not begin and proceed in many of the developing countries until the second half of the twentieth century.

Institution – the manner of organizing and shaping social action within broad spheres of activity, such as in the economy or society, it consists of an array of customs and habits as well as various levels and kinds of specific organizations.

Ku Klux Klan (KKK) – the radical group that emerged in the South after the Civil War, it was designed to eliminate African-Americans, and their sympathizers, through various forms of terror and intimidation. It eventually became very active even in the North, becoming a popular political vehicle in such states as Indiana.

Labor – it can refer both to the producers and to the process whereby goods are created under capitalism.

Landscape – a term that has become popular for depicting the ways in which the constructions of human beings signify the nature of their lives. Used by the urban scholar, Sharon Zukin, it refers to the visual symbols of a city and how they document and portray the lives of the people who live there. Thus, for example, the nature of an old steel mill town is to be found in landscapes in which the tall smoke stacks dominate the skyline on one side, and the display of one-story small wooden houses, occupied by the workers, form the other side of the skyline. The striking difference of the two forms not only is an architectural fact, but it represents the power at work in the community - the dominance of the mill over the lives of the workers.

Market(s) – the system of supply and demand under capitalism whereby goods are produced and distributed.

Metropolis – the dense and extensive concentrations of people, land and buildings, it includes cities plus their suburbs and fringe areas. Today, in the case of a place like New York City, it may include upwards of nine million people, or in the case of Shanghai, as many as 16 million, or even over 20 million in Mexico City.

Neighborhood – the small areas of cities and villages that are characterized by often extensive and intensive social relationships among people. They include both informal ties as well as the clubs and groups that people create.

New Urbanism – the eclectic school of urban theory in the United States that advances the idea that living areas of people must be improved by, among other things, limiting the influence of the automobile and promoting more sites where residents can easily meet and socialize. Some of its model cities include Seaside, Florida and Kentlands, Maryland.

Paradigm – commonly refers to a broad and unique set of theoretical principles that depict the elements and workings of a particular kind of system. In the study of cities one can speak, for example, of a Marxist paradigm insofar as the theory attends to the workings of cities in terms of such elements as the concentration of capital and its impact on the social and political inequalities of residents.

Peripheral city – generally refers to smaller cities located in less developed regions that have a relatively small economic influence on the surrounding areas.

Place – those special sites in space where people live and work. They furnish the basis for a sense of personal identity as well as the grounds on which to establish enduring intimate social relationships.

Pluralism – the school of political theory that claims that different groups – be they social, political, or economic – compete for and carry roughly equal weight in securing power in the political arena.

Post-industrialism – refers to that period in the growth and development of cities after industrialism, characterized by the increasing dominance of the service economy.

Postmodern – refers to a wide-ranging characterization of contemporary life that claims it to be fragmented, chaotic and lacking in a central form or voice of authority, it often is used to describe literature, paintings and even buildings.

Privatism – the term used by the historian, Sam Bass Warner, Jr., to refer to the driving economic forces of the American city; it is the equivalent, for him, of capitalism.

Profane – the concept of Emile Durkheim, used to refer to commonplace, or mundane, activities and their locations. It is the opposite of sacred.

Pueblo – the Spanish term used to depict small villages and towns in countries like Mexico; also means people or nation.

Race – the designation of groups based upon some common definition or physical attributes such as skin color or other features, it is now acknowledged to be the product of states, or dominant groups, that have exercised their power.

Regionalism – a term used to describe the effort to create common programs and activities among different municipal entities within the same general area, such projects are now underway both in the European Union and the United States.

Rentiers – the class of people who own and gain profit from the rent of property and land, of French origin.

Representational spaces – a term used by Henri Lefebrve to depict the creative uses of space in societies, often their forms of art and architecture.

Representations of space – a term used by Henri Lefebrve to refer to the ways in which space was depicted in specific societies, it included such things as maps of the world, of transportation routes and of regions.

Sacred – the term used by the sociologist Emile Durkheim to refer to those objects and sites of special significance in a society, it would include, for instance, both religious temples and the Christian cross.

Segregation – the system whereby people of different racial and ethnic backgrounds tend to live and work in separate areas of cities, with little or no social or physical contact among them.

Social inequality – the inequalities that exist among people in terms of their power and prestige, it often is also associated with their economic inequality, i.e. their differences in wealth and income, as well.

Space – the medium independent of human existence in which there exist objects (including other human beings), objects that behave according to certain basic laws of nature. According to the social philosopher Henri Lefebrve, space can be shaped and influenced by the workings of society, in general, and capitalism, in particular.

Spatial mismatch – the notion used by the sociologist John Kasarda to depict the fact that many of the new and well-paid jobs that arose in American cities after 1970 occurred on the outskirts of the city, while many of those people who needed such jobs the most, in particular, poor African-Americans, lived within the central city. In other words, there was a spatial mismatch of job openings and those who were unemployed.

Spatial practices – the term used by Henri Lefebrve to refer to ways in which the activities of people occurred in space as, for example, the ways in which they went to work or, even, the pace in which they went about their daily routines.

Suburb – those areas on the fringe of dense urban settlements, they arose first around the castles of nobles during the Middle Ages. They became immensely popular in the United States after World War II when many returning war veterans, and their families, set up their first homes. While, at first, mainly the residences of wealthier citizens, today there are many working-class suburbs as well, especially in and around older cities.

Succession – the process whereby one population group is replaced by another in specific areas of cities, it is part of the theoretical imagery used by human ecologists to study and to depict the city.

Sunbelt – a term that became popular after about 1970 in the United States to depict the states of the South and West where many people as well as industries from the older industrial states of the Northeast and Midwest had moved. The term Snowbelt is used to refer to these latter states.

Surplus value – the difference in the value of a commodity between the value that is required to produce that commodity, that is, the value of the labor power, and the value that comes from its exchange in the market, that is, its exchange-value.

The state – the term commonly used by European social theorists to refer to the various political agencies and arms that are empowered to control and regulate the activities of the population. Typically it includes the government, the military and the judiciary. In the work of Karl Marx, the state plays a critical role, largely as a means through which the dominant social class, the bourgeoisie, secured its power over the rest of society. While the

Treaty of Westphalia in 1648 marked the origin of the modern state, the first modern states in Europe did not come into existence until the nineteenth century.

Urban – used to refer to any element or attribute of a dense settlement of people and organization, it often refers simply to cities or metropolitan areas of certain sizes and varying degrees of social diversity and functional specialization.

Use-value – the value of a good to those who use it, the term is used by Karl Marx to distinguish it from exchange-value, or the value of a commodity, something that has value and is exchanged among buyers and sellers. This notion is employed creatively in the theories of cities advanced by David Harvey, and by John Logan and Harvey Molotch.

Value – the worth of a good, either to its user or to its owner.

World-system – a term used by world-system theorists to refer to the capitalist world economic system that is characterized by unequal exchanges of commodities and manufactured goods and unequal distribution of profits among countries located in three hierarchical zones – the core, semi-periphery, and periphery. The core generally includes the United States, the West European states and Japan, while the peripheral countries refer to most of the developing world. The semi-periphery used to refer to the socialist economies of East-Central Europe during the Cold War and has been used to refer to a number of the newly industrializing economies such as Taiwan, South Korea, Brazil, Mexico and so forth. However, members belonging to these categories have changed over time in accordance with the varied criteria used by scholars to classify countries.

Index